Handling stolen goods and theft: A market reduction approach

by Mike Sutton
with assistance from:
Katie Johnston and Heather Lockwood

A Research and Statistics Directorate Report

Home Office
Research and
Statistics
Directorate

London: Home Office

Home Office Research Studies

The Home Office Research Studies are reports on research undertaken by or on behalf of the Home Office. They cover the range of subjects for which the Home Secretary has responsibility. Titles in the series are listed at the back of this report (copies are available from the address on the back cover). Other publications produced by the Research and Statistics Directorate include Research Findings, the Research Bulletin, Statistical Bulletins and Statistical Papers.

The Research and Statistics Directorate

The Directorate consists of units which deal with research and statistics on Crime and Criminal Justice, Offenders and Corrections, Immigration and General Matters; the Programme Development Unit; the Economics Unit; and the Operational Research Unit.

The Research and Statistics Directorate is an integral part of the Home Office, serving the Ministers and the department itself, its services, Parliament and the public through research, development and statistics. Information and knowledge from these sources informs policy development and the management of programmes; their dissemination improves wider public understanding of matters of Home Office concern.

RSD
Research & Statistics Directorate

First published 1998

Application for reproduction should be made to the Information and Publications Group, Room 201, Home Office, 50 Queen Anne's Gate, London SW1H 9AT.

©Crown copyright 1998 ISBN 1 84082 0624
ISSN 0072 6435

Foreword

This report presents findings from the British Crime Survey of the number of people buying stolen goods and their characteristics. In addition, information gathered separately from in-depth interviews with a sample of burglars, other thieves and handlers is used to produce a comprehensive description of the way stolen goods are bought and sold. This is new and valuable information which will further develop crime prevention policy making and stimulate future policing initiatives.

This report contains a number of recommendations for tackling different types of stolen goods markets to reduce theft by reducing demand for stolen goods. The Home Office Police Research Group is currently involved in the implementation and evaluation of a market reduction demonstration project.

CHRIS LEWIS
Head of Offenders and Corrections
Home Office Research and Statistics Directorate

Acknowledgements

I am particularly indebted to John Graham for providing encouragement, valuable advice and suggestions. Thanks for comments on an earlier draft are also due to David Brown, Paul Ekblom, Peter Goldblatt and Malcolm Ramsay. Pat Mayhew, Catriona Mirrlees-Black and Andrew Percy also provided some advice on the BCS data. I would like to thank Donald Roy and Inspector Reg Pengelly for providing items of helpful information. Others helped to find suitable informants and here I am particularly indebted to staff at the Thames Valley Partnership, especially Sue Raikes.

Most importantly, I would like to thank the 45 people who must remain anonymous because they spoke to us at length about their involvement in stealing and with buying and selling stolen goods. Thanks are also due to certain police officers, Prison Service staff, Probation Officers and others who remain anonymous to protect the identity of those we interviewed.

As part of this study, Katie Johnston interviewed 10 drug users attending a methadone treatment clinic and six young people from a juvenile motor crime project. Heather Lockwood also assisted. She wrote the case studies in Appendix 4 from recordings of earlier interviews. Professor Mike Maguire provided previously unpublished material from work conducted with Douglas Webster in the early 1970s (Appendix 3).

This study was subject to an independent peer review by Professor Nick Tilley of Nottingham Trent University.

MIKE SUTTON

Glossary of terms

ACORN   Neighbourhood classification based on data from the Census, used predominantly by marketers and planners in Great Britain for profiling purchasing and lifestyle behaviour.

Adverse area factors   These three factors (ACORN category, drug problems in neighbourhood and burglaries committed by locals) were derived from logistic regression models and were independently correlated with buying stolen goods.

Adverse personal wealth factors   These three factors (lost wage, not managing on income and not having contents insurance) were derived from logistic regression models and were independently correlated with buying stolen goods.

Commercial fence   Retailer dealing in stolen property from commercial premises.

Crack   Cocaine rocks.

Fence   A dealer in stolen property

Forward stepwise method   Logistic regression procedure for entering variables into a model (see Logistic regression).

Hawking   Selling goods, door to door, around pubs and clubs or on the street.

Kiting   To issue fictitious papers to obtain credit or money. Thieves often refer to the use of stolen cheque books and credit cards as 'kiting'.

Logistic regression Using this statistical technique you analyse data to estimate directly the probability of a particular event occurring.

Multivariate analysis Statistical procedure, such as Logistic regression, that allows for the examination of many variables together and takes into account the correlations among variables.

Residential fence Neighbourhood dealer in stolen goods operating from their own home or lock-up garage.

Situational crime prevention Comprises opportunity-reduction measures that are directed at specific forms of crime. Measures are directed at design or manipulation of the immediate environment to increase the effort and risks of crime while reducing the rewards.

Smack Slang for heroin.

Typology Study of types or the correspondence between them.

Contents

Summary

The purpose of this report is to explore the effects of the market for stolen goods on levels of acquisitive crime. It examines the possibility of reducing demand and supply in criminal markets as a new method of crime control.

The study is based upon information obtained from the British Crime Survey (BCS) and in-depth interviews with thieves and other handlers of stolen goods. It examines the nature and extent of the stolen goods problem and reveals commonly used and successful methods of selling stolen goods. The study, which deals with offender motivation as well as the vulnerability of victims' possessions, found that markets for stolen goods have considerable influence upon decisions to begin and continue stealing.

The Market Reduction Approach, proposed in this study, aims to reduce stolen goods markets by discouraging people from dealing in them. It incorporates crime prevention methods designed to reduce opportunities for crime, while tackling an important underlying 'social cause' of theft.

Extent of the stolen goods problem

The BCS revealed that a large number of people are offered as well as buy stolen goods. Those living in poorer areas are more likely to be offered stolen goods and buy them, and many more believe that their neighbours own stolen goods.

Findings from the BCS show that many members of the public knowingly buy stolen goods:

- 11 percent of BCS respondents admitted buying stolen goods in the past five years.

- 70 percent thought that some of their neighbours had stolen goods such as VCRs and TVs in their homes.

- Almost half of males aged 16-24 believed they had been offered or bought stolen goods.

- More than twice as many males are offered stolen goods as females and nearly twice as many males buy stolen goods.

- 30 percent of all males living in areas characterised by three adverse area factors, and 40 percent of all males with three adverse personal wealth factors, knowingly bought what they thought to be stolen goods.

- Living in a household where the head was self-employed significantly increased the likelihood of respondents saying they had bought stolen goods. This finding was supported by in-depth interviews which revealed that small business owners are repeatedly targeted by thieves asking them to buy stolen goods.

Stolen goods markets

- Stolen property markets are for the most part like other illegal markets: localised, fragmented, ephemeral and undiversified[1].

- Different types of stolen goods are sold in particular ways. Jewellery is usually sold to jewellers' shops. Car stereos are often sold to Residential Fences and then through networks of friends; stolen cheque books and credit cards are often sold to those who frequently use drugs; shoplifters sell clothes and food door-to-door or around pubs. Stolen cars - even those only a few years old - are frequently sold to car breakers' yards.

Prices

- Second-hand items are usually sold by thieves for a third of the retail value. If the thief sells to a Residential Fence, the fence usually sells the item(s) to a consumer for half the retail value. Goods sold to second-hand shops are usually sold on to the public for two thirds of the retail value. Thieves selling gold jewellery to jewellery shops are paid the going rate for scrap gold.

- Stolen goods are not always sold to consumers for less than the retail price. A Commercial Fence can sell stolen jewellery in their jeweller's

---

1   See Reuter 1995.

shop for the same price as legitimate jewellery. Corner shop owners can do the same with packaged goods.

Issues of supply and demand

- When new products such as video cassette recorders, mobile telephones, personal computers or camcorders come on the market, they are frequently targeted by thieves because they are state-of-the-art, desirable and expensive. It is easier to find buyers for these products among those who cannot afford or are unwilling to pay high street prices.

- Small business owners are frequently offered stolen goods by people they have never met before.

- Particularly active and efficient fences tend to encourage thieves to increase their offending.

- Experienced and prolific thieves, particularly the drug users interviewed, were proactive in finding new buyers and sold to a large number of different people. By doing so they were better able to overcome any fluctuations in their local stolen goods markets. This also meant they were able to sell quickly if they were not in close proximity to their usual buyers, thus minimising their risk of arrest because they only needed to transport stolen goods short distances to buyers close to the scene of the crime.

- Inexperienced thieves tend to rely on existing markets, particularly a single Residential Fence who is usually either a relative or neighbour.

- Stealing to order is done by experienced and inexperienced thieves alike and is particularly common in shoplifting, car stereo theft and school, factory, warehouse and office burglaries. It seems that domestic burglars rarely steal to order.

- Those involved in frequent use of illegal drugs are much more likely to take risks and accept lower returns for stolen goods.

Crime and criminality prevention issues

- Car stereos with a clip-off face or pull-out design are supposed to be less attractive to thieves, but these were undoubtedly the most sought-after car stereos. Even when they had been removed, thieves broke into cars in the hope of finding them either under the seat, or in the glove box or luggage compartment.

- Property marking did not deter thieves from stealing marked items. Neither did it deter others from buying and selling marked goods.

- For the novice thief, the experience of success or failure to convert stolen property into cash appears to play an important part in whether they continue to offend. This is an important area for crime prevention. Reducing markets for stolen goods might curtail many criminal careers before they 'take off'.

- The use of taxis to transport burglars and stolen goods appears to be widespread.

- Contrary to popular belief, none of those interviewed sold stolen goods at car boot sales or thought that stolen goods were sold in this way.

The Market Reduction Approach

- Stolen goods markets not only support the thieves themselves, they also provide illegal gain for a whole stratum of people supplying 'criminal services', and of course, for consumers. The key new principle of the Market Reduction Approach, proposed in this study, is that it does not focus merely upon specific theft situations or specific thieves. Instead, it seeks to deal with the market and the players in it who affect many situations and many thieves by providing incentives and incitement for theft.

- The Market Reduction Approach involves reducing demand and supply in the five main stolen goods markets identified in this study. It addresses an important underlying cause of theft and provides a new route for utilising the effectiveness of existing crime prevention measures.

1 Introduction

Buying or selling stolen goods (handling) is an offence under the Theft Act 1968. Section 22(1) of the Act requires guilt to be established on the basis of 'knowledge' or 'belief' that goods were stolen. Estimates based on official crime statistics and figures from the BCS suggest that, in Britain in 1995, thieves selling stolen property cleared between £900 million and £1680 million (net) and that fences cleared between £450 million and £870 million (net) through selling stolen property.[2]

An earlier review of the literature found that very little has been written about the factors which influence demand for stolen goods (Sutton 1993). There has been little research to determine how and where goods are disposed of, or how often and in what circumstances people are offered stolen goods. Further, there has been little research to date on the roles played by thieves, fences and consumers in the overall redistribution of stolen goods. Research has not examined whether the existence of a market for stolen goods provides motivation for theft and influences what is actually stolen, or whether the pervasive market for stolen goods influences the rate of burglary and other acquisitive crimes. There have been no nationally representative surveys of prevalence of buying stolen goods among the public, although the Youth Lifestyles Survey (Graham and Bowling 1995) found the most common offences committed by young offenders were buying or selling stolen goods. Since burglary and theft are considered such important social problems, it is odd that these factors have been so neglected by criminologists. This is an area where more research might open up new avenues for reducing acquisitive crime levels by tackling an important underlying social and economic cause of theft.

To fill in some of the gaps in our knowledge, this study looks in detail at the buying and selling process in terms of the concepts of supply and demand as well as other factors that influence markets for stolen goods. The 1994 British Crime Survey (BCS) asked about buying and being offered stolen goods. Responses are examined to find out more about the social and

---

2   UK National Accounts. Unpublished Office of National Statistics document.

demographic characteristics of buyers. The BCS data are also examined to find out more about why certain people get offered stolen goods; the effect of self-employment; neighbourhood; gender; age and carrying large amounts of cash. This information is used to identify where, and at whom, particular crime prevention strategies might best be aimed.

In addition to the BCS data, this study includes results from 45 in-depth interviews conducted with thieves and buyers of stolen goods. Findings from these interviews are used to examine several important yet under-researched aspects of the market for stolen goods: whether buyers provide motivation for others to steal; whether this influences what is actually stolen and whether an increase in demand for stolen goods leads to an increase in theft. How an offender's knowledge of particular markets for stolen goods, and access to these markets, plays an important part in offending is also examined.

Previous studies of burglars have looked at what they do with stolen goods - particularly their relationships with fences (Maguire 1982; Wright and Decker 1994). Others have concentrated upon the dealings of one particular fence (Klockars 1974; Steffensmeier, 1986). This, however, is the first research study to look in depth at stolen goods markets and how they operate. It reveals estimates of the extent to which members of the public have bought stolen goods in their daily lives, the background factors associated with buying and being offered stolen goods, and how these factors influence motives and opportunities within each of the identified five stolen goods markets.

Outline and Structure of the Report

Chapter 2 looks at the nature and extent of the stolen goods problem. Findings from the BCS are examined to determine some important demographic characteristics of buyers.

Chapter 3 provides a typology of buyers and sellers and looks in more detail at the type of people who deal with them. This chapter presents some results from the BCS and identifies particular adverse area and personal factors associated with buying stolen goods. Wider purchasing patterns of buyers are also examined.

Chapter 4 provides a typology of stolen goods markets. Using findings from the in-depth interviews, five different types of market are described, along with examples of how stolen goods are bought and sold within them.

Stolen goods markets share many of the characteristics of other types of market. Chapter 5 looks at how stolen goods markets operate. The roles of entrepreneurs and criminal careers are examined. This chapter also discusses the way thieves cultivate markets for stolen goods and how, in turn, stolen goods markets provide an incentive for theft. Other issues considered are whether an increase in demand for particular stolen goods affects what is actually stolen and whether this then leads to an increase in theft. Considering the importance of price in the marketing of stolen goods, this chapter also looks at the price thieves get, and the percentage of the retail price paid by fences and other members of the public for stolen goods. Some insights are provided into the ways stolen goods are exchanged for drugs and what else thieves do with the proceeds of crime.

Chapter 6 reveals some of the ways in which stolen goods markets are different from other types of market, and explains some of these distinguishing characteristics.

Chapter 7 looks at what happens to stolen goods. Examples are provided for car stereos, jewellery, cheques and credit cards.

Chapter 8 discusses the main findings of this study. It considers the influence of property marking, target hardening and other situational approaches to crime prevention on thieves' decisions about what to steal.

Finally, Chapter 9 outlines how particular situational crime prevention approaches might work to reduce each of the main stolen goods markets.

The samples and their limitations

This report is based on information obtained from the BCS and in-depth interviews with thieves and other handlers of stolen goods. The BCS sample is taken from a total of 9646 respondents, aged between 16 and 59, who answered a number of self-reported offending questions in the 1994 BCS. Some 241 respondents refused to answer these questions. Those aged 60 or more were screened out by the interviewer because it was felt 'techno-fear' of the laptop computer might bias the responses of older respondents. Among the younger age group, 893 respondents felt unable to use the computer themselves to answer the self-report questions and needed assistance from the interviewer. They were excluded from this analysis on the same grounds.[3]

For some of the analysis, data are weighted to nationally representative levels

---

3   The self-keying use of the laptop by the respondent was meant to help them feel more confident that the information they gave would be treated confidentially. It was felt that self-report questions completed in this way might be different from those completed with the assistance of the interviewer.

because the BCS sample was not totally random.[4] The total unweighted BCS sample used for this report was 8753.[5]

Research technique

The Computer Assisted Personal Interviewing technique (CAPI) was used for the first time in the 1994 BCS. The automatic routing and error checking of the CAPI system is designed to minimise interviewer and respondent error and so improve data quality. It involved interviewers using a laptop computer to display the BCS questionnaire and directly type in respondents' answers. At certain times the computer was turned around so that respondents keyed their own answers to a series of questions. This self-keying CAPI system successfully recorded responses to questions about purchasing of stolen goods that had previously been dogged by a high refusal rate. These questions had caused difficulties for both interviewers and respondents when piloted with a traditional paper questionnaire, possibly because many respondents were using the property in their own homes and either felt embarrassed or, despite assurances of confidentiality, feared subsequent prosecution.

In-depth interviews

The 45 in-depth interviews were conducted with a mixture of people who have been involved in buying or selling stolen goods at different levels and to various degrees. They include: 14 respondents who were followed-up from the Youth Lifestyles Survey (YLS),[6] 10 from a Young Offender Institution (YOI), four from adult male prisons, seven from the Probation Service and a total of 10 heroin addicts (or ex-addicts) from two methadone treatment clinics in the Greater London area.[7]

The in-depth sample was not intended to be representative, or reflect all types of participants involved in redistributing stolen goods. As this type of sampling is not designed to generalise to the whole population (unlike the BCS), the method used is intended to indicate common links or categories between those interviewed and others like them. The interviews provide detailed information on a small number of individuals, rather than a limited amount of information on a larger number.

It should be emphasised that this part of the study is based on retrospective,

---

4   For instance, those in inner city areas were over sampled (see Mayhew et al 1993: 157).
5   The BCS uses probability sampling and weights the data to ensure that certain elements of the population (e.g. those living in the inner city or not) have an equal chance of inclusion (see Ramsay and Percy 1994). The ethnic booster sample of 1527 respondents (see Mayhew et al 1993: 7) was not analysed in this study.
6   (Graham and Bowling 1995).
7   See Appendix 2 for further details.

subjective accounts from interviewees who supplied their own reconstructions of events. These will be affected by the respondent's memory. They provide, however, an extremely useful personal perspective which is helpful in interpreting and explaining the facts portrayed by statistical data.

Research of this kind is useful for finding out the 'thieves' story', establishing their motives and improving our understanding of how they operate. It provides new insights while occasionally casting doubt on perceived wisdom. For instance, despite much speculation in the national press, none of those interviewed had sold stolen goods at car boot sales or thought that such goods were sold in this way. However, there may be some local variations in the way stolen goods markets operate and these will not be picked up by a sample of this kind. Additionally, more specialised markets such as those for stolen art and rare antiques are not described.

An interview schedule ensured coverage of certain themes which emerged from an earlier review of the literature (Sutton 1993, 1995), and the BCS. Every interview was fully tape-recorded and transcribed into a text-based thematic data set on a computer. All statements presented in this report are taken verbatim from these transcripts. No time limit was imposed for the interviews. The shortest took 35 minutes and the longest took two and a half hours. On average, they took 90 minutes to complete.

The young people followed up from the YLS comprised eight males and six females in their late teens and early twenties. They included young people who only bought and sold once or twice, and others who, despite being in regular employment, had seized many opportunities to make money from buying and selling stolen goods. Although three people (two male, one female) had spent periods in adult prisons for theft, burglary, and dealing in drugs, their involvement in offending was generally not as persistent and extensive as those from the YOI or adult prisons. Their offending more often involved shoplifting, theft from work, theft from unoccupied dwelling houses or schools, and only occasionally burglaries of dwelling houses. Three young people from this sample had been looked after in local authority residential homes as a result of family problems and their own delinquency. One remained a heroin and cocaine user and continued to deal in drugs from her home despite having been arrested many times, serving terms of imprisonment and probation. Two interviewees declined to talk about their own buying and selling behaviour but spoke in some depth about how friends and associates bought and sold stolen goods.

The male offenders from a YOI were aged between 17 and 21 and were selected on the basis of their extensive involvement in acquisitive crime. One had been involved in a large number of street robberies (for which he had not been caught) and convicted for rape. Another was a member of a gang that had been involved in a series of ram raids and office burglaries - including thefts of designer clothes, computers and computer memory chips. Others had committed many burglaries and car thefts. Most of these young men had parents and siblings who were also offenders and had been imprisoned. Some clearly referred to themselves as villains or burglars and expressed no intention of giving up crime on their release.

The four male offenders (aged 22, 26, 28 and 50) serving sentences in adult training prisons were also selected on the basis of their extensive involvement in property crime. Two had been frequent drug users and were in a drug rehabilitation unit. All were serving sentences ranging between three and nine years for burglary.

With the co-operation of the Probation Service, interviews were conducted at a motor project for young people involved in car crime. A total of six males (there were no females), aged between 14 and 22, agreed to be interviewed alone and talked candidly about their involvement in joy riding, theft of car stereo systems and car theft. They appeared to be on the verge of engaging in the same level and degree of crime as those in the YOI. However, their lives were somewhat more stable. Although they were residing in high crime neighbourhoods, they tended to live still with one or both parents (as opposed to being in local authority care, or living with friends or relatives). One (aged 22), had been involved in more serious car crime, which had escalated to the point of stealing and delivering stolen cars to order. One interview was also conducted, at a probation office, with a 31-year-old man who had a long history of car crime but had resolved to stop offending following a four-year term of imprisonment for stealing cars.

The heroin users were interviewed at two different methadone treatment centres in the south of England. This sample, comprising eight males and two females, was drawn with the assistance of the staff at the clinics. The staff knew many of the patients well and identified those with lengthy histories of acquisitive crime who would be prepared to talk openly about how they financed their extensive past drug use. All had been involved in drug dealing for a number of years, as well as shoplifting, burglary, cheque and credit card fraud, and buying and selling stolen goods. They had quite extensive experience of the criminal justice system, and five had served sentences at adult prisons for burglary and shoplifting. Their ages ranged from 19 to 44 years.

2 Nature and extent of the stolen goods problem

This chapter examines how many people buy stolen goods and how frequently they make such purchases. Looking at associations between age, gender and types of housing area, it also focuses on the relationship between beliefs about neighbours buying stolen goods and respondents' own purchasing behaviour. Readers should be aware that these figures are representative of people who bought goods that they either knew or believed to be stolen and cannot account for stolen goods purchases made by 'innocent' consumers from unscrupulous shopkeepers or other members of the public.

Incidence of handling stolen goods

In England and Wales in 1995, 41,568 handling[8] stolen goods offences were recorded by the police. There were 34,021 prosecutions with 22,964 resulting in a successful conviction. Table 2.1 displays the figures for those aged over 16. Considerably more males were prosecuted than females and more younger males were prosecuted than any other group.

Table 2.1 Percentage prosecuted and convicted for handling stolen goods by age group and gender

	Men				Women			
	16-24	25-35	36-59	60+	16-24	25-35	36-59	60+
N Prosecuted	(13435)	(9936)	(4079)	(130)	(2143)	(1976)	(726)	(27)
	%	%	%	%	%	%	%	%
Prosecuted †	41	31	13	<1	7	6	2	<1
Convicted ‡	68	67	69	62	67	70	60	33

Source - Home Office court statistics 1995. † Percentage of all handling prosecutions. ‡ Percentage convicted within age and gender group prosecuted.

---

8   Possessing stolen goods - buying, selling or storing.

In the nationally representative BCS, respondents were asked: "How often have you purchased things you believed to be stolen in the past five years?".[9] Eleven percent of the sample said they had bought stolen goods at least once (Table 2.2).

Table 2.2 Frequency of buying stolen goods in past five years

	%	Unweighted N
Never	88.5	7734
Once	5.5	475
A few times	5.3	480
Often	0.5	51
Don't know	<0.5	1
Refused	<0.5	12
Total		8753

Weighted data. Source: 1994 BCS, core sample, CAPI respondents.

Thus, more than one in 10 of the population in England and Wales aged between 16 and 60 have bought items which they either knew or believed to be stolen goods. However, this figure is likely to be an underestimate because some respondents will have been reluctant to admit to buying stolen goods and others may have forgotten (see Walker 1983).

There are clear age and gender differences in buying behaviour. A greater proportion of those aged between 16 and 24 bought stolen goods and almost twice as many males bought stolen goods as females (Table 2.3).

Table 2.3 Buying stolen goods by age group and gender

	Men			Women		
	16-24	25-35	36-59	16-24	25-35	36-59
N	(600)	(1266)	(2161)	(763)	(1677)	(2286)
	%	%	%	%	%	%
Bought	**31**	16	7	**17**	10	5

Weighted percentages. Unweighted N = 8753 Source: 1994 BCS, core sample, CAPI respondents.

Housing areas

Different types of urban environment are characterised by particular types of crime and offenders (Park, Burgess and Mckenzie 1925; Baldwin and Bottoms 1976). Table 2.4 looks at the relationship between the area where respondents live and buying stolen goods. In this table, housing areas are distinguished using the ACORN classification system. ACORN was primarily

---

9   These questions followed those concerned with general purchasing patterns.

developed for market research purposes - to enable fine-grade consumer analysis - and is based upon Census variables. ACORN categories have been particularly effective in interpreting BCS data in the past (see Mayhew et al 1989; Hough, 1995). **Thriving** areas are the most affluent and house those defined as: Wealthy Achievers in suburban areas; Affluent Greys (i.e. affluent senior citizens) in rural communities and Prosperous Pensioners in retirement areas. **Expanding** areas house those defined as Affluent Executives and Well-Off Workers living in family areas. **Rising** areas contain Affluent Urbanites in town and city areas, Prosperous Professionals in metropolitan areas and Better-Off Executives living in Inner City Areas. **Settling** areas are comprised of people classified as Comfortable Middle Agers in mature home-owning areas and Skilled Workers in home-owning areas. **Aspiring** areas are characterised by New Home Owners in mature communities and White Collar Workers living in better-off multi-ethnic areas. **Striving** areas are the least well-off. They represent older people in less prosperous areas, council estate residents in better-off homes, areas of high unemployment or areas of greatest hardship and people in multi-ethnic low-income areas.

Within England and Wales, 20 percent of the population live in Thriving areas, 10.3 percent in Expanding, 9.1 percent in Rising, 25.5 percent in Settling, 14 percent in Aspiring and 21.1 percent in Striving.

Table 2.4 ACORN categories by buying stolen goods

	Thriving	Expanding	Rising	Settling	Aspiring	Striving
N	(1499)	(1053)	(758)	(2218)	(1154)	(2071)
	%	%	%	%	%	%
Bought	7	9	12	11	12	**17**

Weighted data. Unweighted n = 8753. Source: 1994 BCS, core sample.

The bulk (60%) of the population live in Expanding, Rising, Settling and Aspiring ACORN areas. Within each of these areas the populations are heterogeneous. By contrast, the populations of Thriving and Striving areas are homogenous. This clearer distinction between the two extreme ACORN area types explains a particularly notable difference between the Thriving and Striving categories: more than twice as many of those living in the less well-off Striving areas bought stolen goods, compared with those in affluent Thriving areas.

Neighbours

BCS respondents were also asked: "How many people in this area do you think have got stolen goods in their homes, such as tv sets or video recorders?" A large proportion (70%) thought that some of their neighbours owned stolen goods and 21 percent thought that at least quite a few of their neighbours did (Table 2.5).

Table 2.5 *Percentage of respondents believing others in neighbourhood have stolen goods in their homes*

	%	Unweighted N
A Lot	4	408
Quite a few	17	1588
Not very many	49	4217
None at all	27	2210
Don't Know	<1	13
Refused	3	317
Total	100	8753

Weighted data. Source: 1994 BCS core sample

Table 2.6 shows how belief about the level of neighbours' ownership of stolen goods corresponds with self-reported buying. Clearly, a much larger proportion of BCS respondents thought their neighbours owned stolen goods than admitted to buying themselves. This is a difficult finding to explain and could be due to a number of reasons including reluctance to report their own buying of stolen goods. Considerably more respondents who thought that a lot or quite a few of their neighbours had stolen goods admitted to buying themselves. It seems reasonable to conclude that those who buy stolen goods are more likely to live in neighbourhoods where at least 'quite a few' other people also own stolen goods. However, these figures need to be treated cautiously because it is not known how accurately belief about neighbours' ownership of stolen goods reflects real levels of ownership among neighbours. Rather than stemming from any real impression or knowledge of neighbours owning stolen goods, it is possible that some respondents said that neighbours own stolen goods simply because they themselves had purchased them; or alternatively, because they had an exaggerated fear of crime and criminality in their neighbourhood.

Table 2.6 *How many people in area have stolen goods*

	a lot	a few	not many	none	refused	d.know
	%	%	%	%	%	%
Bought stolen goods						
yes	29	26	10	4	0	6
no	71	74	90	96	100	94
Total	100	100	100	100	100	100
Unweighted n	408	1588	4217	2210	13	317

Weighted data. Unweighted n = 8753 Source:1994 BCS, core sample.

There is a marked difference between residents in the affluent Thriving ACORN areas and the poorer Striving areas in terms of belief about how many neighbours own stolen goods. As Table 2.7 shows, four times more of those living in Striving areas believe that a lot or quite a few of their neighbours have stolen goods in their homes.

Table 2.7 *Percentage of respondents believing others in neighbourhood have stolen goods in their homes by ACORN*

N	Thriving (1499)	Expanding (1053)	Rising (758)	Settling (2218)	Aspiring (1154)	Striving (2071)
	%	%	%	%	%	%
A Lot	1	3	4	3	3	**10**
Quite a few	8	13	21	14	19	**28**
Not very many	50	52	50	54	49	39
None at all	39	30	21	26	24	18
Don't know	<1	0	<1	<1	<1	<1
Refused	2	3	4	3	5	4

Weighted data. Unweighted n = 8753 Source: 1994 BCS, core sample.

Summary and Conclusions

While most people in Britain generally agree that stealing is wrong, at least 11 percent admit to having bought stolen goods in the last five years. Comparing males with females, more than twice as many males buy.

Burglars and other thieves most often live in poorer housing areas and since the opportunity to knowingly buy stolen goods depends upon meeting or knowing someone willing to sell (rather than buying unwittingly from a shop), people living in these areas are correspondingly more likely than people living in more affluent areas to knowingly own stolen goods. Therefore, people living in poorer areas where there is a more plentiful supply of stolen goods will also have quite a few, or even a lot, of neighbours who know they have stolen goods in their homes. Further, buying stolen goods is closely related to friendship and neighbourhood networks where "word of mouth" plays an important part in the distribution process (see Foster, 1990). This means it is likely that people who buy stolen goods in this way would know that certain neighbours had also bought them.

As Table 2.5 shows, many more people (70%) think that some of their neighbours own stolen goods than admitted to buying stolen goods themselves. This is an important finding because this general belief about ownership levels could be utilised by crime prevention strategies encouraging intolerance towards markets for stolen goods. Many people fear being burgled or having things stolen from their cars (Hough 1995), so there may be considerable scope for reducing the demand for stolen goods by increasing the public's awareness of the links between markets for stolen goods and theft.

The propensity of those living in poorer areas to buy and own stolen goods may be of interest to wider debates about poverty and social exclusion. Survey results of household expenditure (e.g. Goodman and Webb 1995, DSS 1996, Goodman et al 1997) have found that a significant proportion of those in the lowest income group spend more on consumer durables than others with higher incomes. And this has been used to refute evidence, based solely on income, that the real income of low income households has not risen since the late 1970s. It now seems that a partial explanation for the disparity between income and spending, amongst the least well off, may be due to expenditure on stolen goods such as video recorders, mobile telephones and television sets.[10]

---

10   Assuming that expenditure survey respondents provide figures for the retail value of stolen goods bought rather than the actual amount paid.

3 BUYERS AND SELLERS OF STOLEN GOODS

This chapter includes a brief discussion of what it means to be a 'fence' for stolen goods and how the term 'fence' is defined and understood. It also provides a typology of buyers and sellers of stolen goods and considers purchasing patterns and some of the social characteristics of buyers. These are identified using self-report data alongside other measures.

Earlier typologies of buyers and sellers of stolen goods

The literature on stolen goods contains several different classifications and definitions of those who buy and sell stolen goods. At one extreme, the term 'fence' has been interpreted to mean someone who is law-abiding in most other respects but who on one occasion succumbs to temptation and buys, for example, a stolen television (Shover 1972). At the other extreme, it has been limited to full-time dealers in stolen goods (Klockars 1974).

Steffensmeier's (1986) definition of the fence is particularly subtle:

> "...someone who purchases stolen goods both on a regular basis, and for resale. He [sic] is above all a *reliable outlet for prospective thieves*. The critical features of this definition are that the fence has direct contact with thieves, he buys and resells stolen goods *regularly and persistently*, in so doing he becomes a *public* dealer -recognised as a fence by thieves, the police, and others acquainted with the criminal community."

The fence studied by Steffensmeir operated from a business premises and so his definition does not include the less visible dealers in stolen goods who operate from their own homes or lock-up garages.[11] Other writers have developed a classification which avoids the use of the term 'fence'

---

11   Police searching lock-up garages in London in 1997 for an IRA cache of the explosive Semtex found (as an unexpected bonus) more than £1m worth of stolen goods (The Independent, 3 July 1997).

altogether. Hall (1952) distinguishes between Lay Receivers, Occasional Receivers and Professional Receivers. Cromwell and McElrath (1994) use similar terms. They identify three levels of receiver: Professional, Avocational and Amateur. They define the Professional receiver as someone whose principal enterprise is buying and selling stolen property. The Professional may deal in stolen goods as well as run a legitimate business with legitimate stock that is compatible with the stolen goods they handle. Avocational receivers may also run a business - and for them buying and selling stolen goods is not their principal livelihood. Amateur receivers are described as otherwise honest citizens who buy stolen property on a relatively small scale, primarily but not exclusively for personal consumption.

The main limitation with the typologies adopted by Hall (1952) and Cromwell and McElrath (1994) is that it is difficult to determine whether so-called 'professional receivers' make most of their money through handling stolen goods or through their legitimate enterprise. The extent to which one or the other contributes to income may also vary periodically. Receivers sometimes rely solely upon handling stolen goods for their income and do not have any source of legitimate income. Indeed, they may also engage in stealing.

The following section describes a classification system of buyers and sellers of stolen goods which avoids the need to establish the extent to which dealing in stolen goods contributes to income. This is developed further in Chapter 4 to describe different stolen goods markets.

A typology of buyers and sellers of stolen goods

A useful way to begin to understand the distribution process of stolen goods is to classify those who are involved as either consumers or distributors[12] (See fig 3.1).

Consumers - may make the odd foray into petty stealing or have broken into buildings once or twice when younger. They mainly:

- steal and buy stolen goods for personal consumption only *(Consumer I)*

- buy stolen goods for personal consumption but do not steal *(Consumer II)*

- steal for personal consumption only, but do not buy stolen goods *(Consumer III)*

---

12   This classification was initially conceived following the first 25 in-depth interviews conducted in this study.

Distributors - may occasionally keep some things for personal use[13] but mainly:

- buy stolen goods to sell, or sell for commission, but do not steal *(Distributor I)*

- steal to sell and also buy to sell. May, on rare occasions, also sell on a commission basis for other thieves *(Distributor II)*

- steal to sell, but do not buy stolen goods to sell. However, may occasionally sell stolen goods, on a commission basis, for other thieves *(Distributor III)*

Figure 3.1 *Distributors and consumers of stolen goods*

DISTRIBUTORS SELL STOLEN GOODS TO CONSUMERS

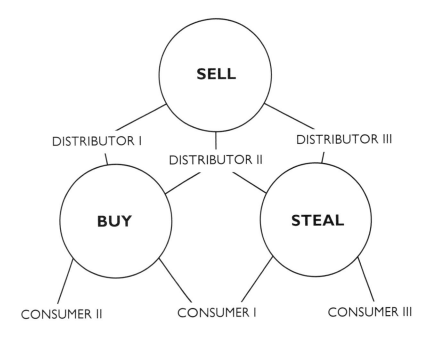

CONSUMERS KEEP STOLEN GOODS

---

13 Several interviewees said this was a high risk strategy. They preferred to sell stolen goods and use the money to buy new goods - for which they could produce a receipt whenever their houses were searched by police officers.

The qualitative sample contains only four pure consumers. Consumers were expected in the sample of interviewees who had participated in the YLS, but only one was identified from this source.[14] Three more consumers were interviewed from Probation Service motor projects. These four were younger and were by far the least criminogenic of the sample. In total, therefore, the sample comprises three *Consumer I* and one *Consumer II*. The rest of the qualitative sample were distributors:[15] five *Distributor I*; 22 *Distributor II*; and 12 *Distributor III*. Two respondents refused to speak about their own buying, selling and stealing behaviour and so could not be classified.

Purchasing patterns as indirect measures of buying stolen goods

Despite the use of CAPI in the BCS, it was felt that reluctance to answer questions about purchasing stolen goods would be high due to concerns about possible repercussions.[16] Therefore, BCS respondents who said they had bought stolen goods were not directly asked questions such as what stolen goods they had bought, or where they had bought them from. They were, however, asked about purchasing methods in a way that would identify purchases made under what might be described as shady or 'dodgy' circumstances. This is how it was done. Firstly, they were asked if they owned any of the following - bicycle, colour television, video cassette recorder (VCR), hi-fi, car stereo (cassette or CD), mobile phone, camera, jewellery. These items were chosen because they are known to be commonly taken by domestic burglars and other thieves. Respondents were then asked if they had purchased any of these in the past 12 months and, for each item bought, how it had been purchased - from a shop/catalogue, second-hand from a shop, or at a pub, for example. Figure 3.2 shows how these questions were routed.

Asking respondents in this way produced a very low refusal rate. Less than one percent said they did not know or refused to say how they had purchased goods bought in the past 12 months. This is a considerable improvement on the 10 percent refusal rate when asked directly if they had bought stolen goods in the past five years.

---

14 The main reason for this is that the YLS did not distinguish between buyers and sellers of stolen goods - and so it was not possible to select a purposive sample of consumers from the data set. Respondents were invited to participate if they had committed three or more acquisitive crimes including buying or selling stolen goods.

15 Apart from two young people from the YLS who retracted what they had said two years earlier, maintaining they had not actually been involved in offending - yet spoke at some length about friends and people they knew who were involved.

16 Although CAPI almost certainly increased the response rate to sensitive questions, 10 percent of respondents still refused to answer or said they did not know if they had bought stolen goods (see Walker 1983).

Figure 3.2

Table 3.1 Purchasing patterns

	Colour TV	VCR	Stereo/ Hi-fi	Car Stereo	Mobile Phone	Bicycle	Jewels [17]	Camera
	%	%	%	%	%	%	%	%
New from shop or catalogue	84	84	88	73	82	75	95	91
Some other way	16	16	12	27	18	25	5	9
Don't know/ Refused	<1	<1	<1	0	0	<1	<1	0
Unweighted N	1735	1461	1823	1047	481	1516	3413	1416

Weighted data. Source: 1994 BCS, core sample, CAPI respondents.
Based on those who had purchased items in past 12 months aged 16-59

17   Jewellery of the kind bought in a jeweller's shop - not just cheaper costume jewellery.

Many respondents purchased at least one of the eight key consumer durables (72 percent) in the past 12 months. Not surprisingly, most bought new items from either a shop or catalogue. Looking at the core sample of CAPI respondents,[18] 67 percent purchased at least one item new from a shop or catalogue. However, 17 percent purchased at least one in some other way. Turning to those who purchased at least one item in the past year,[19] 15 percent bought at least one item new from a shop or catalogue and at least one other some other way; eight percent bought some other way only and 77 percent new from a shop or catalogue only. That is, 23 percent bought at least one item some other way.[20]

Table 3.2 Purchasing patterns: other than new from shop or catalogue

	Colour TV	VCR	Stereo/ Hi-fi	Car Stereo	Mobile Phone	Bicycle	Jewels	Camera
	%	%	%	%	%	%	%	%
Small adds.	14	12	17	11	10	29	7	7
Markets+	4	4	6	8	2	10	15	13
Pub/club	<1	<1	<1	<1	0	<1	2	2
At home	6	3	6	2	4	5	5	4
Shop	28	24	10	9	8	18	19	19
Yet another way	47	56	61	69	76	38	51	56
Unweigt. N	306	238	245	292	82	389	168	136

Weighted data. Source: 1994 BCS, core sample. Based on those who had purchased items in past 12 months. +Includes boot sales and fairs.

Table 3.2 shows where the eight key consumer durables bought some other way were purchased. Of those who bought goods some other way, the most common method was *in yet another way again*. In fact, over nine percent[21] of the BCS respondents had bought at least one of the eight key consumer durables yet another way in the past 12 months. This was a surprising finding because, apart from buying at work (legally), it is difficult to think of any legal way of buying yet another way. Yet, outside of shops and catalogues, this was the most common method of purchasing more than half the items listed. Some of these goods may not have been stolen but purchased within a wider informal economy involving pirated goods and VAT evasion. However, it seems likely that many people who bought goods yet another way would have *knowingly* bought these items as stolen goods, either through friendship networks, directly from thieves over the doorstep, or in pubs and other places.[22] It also seems likely that many of those who said they had bought at a pub or club, or at home, had bought these items as stolen goods. Combining those who purchased items at home, in a pub or club or yet another way in the past 12 months with those who admitted

18   Including buyers and non-buyers of the eight core consumer durables. Weighted data, unweighted N = 8753.
19   Weighted data, unweighted N = 6173.
20   Weighted data, unweighted N=1458.
21   9.4% (weighted data), N = 808 (unweighted).
22   These methods of buying are discussed in detail later in the study.

buying stolen goods in the past five years, 14 percent can be classified as *risky buyers*.[23]

The characteristics of buyers of stolen goods

To understand more about the reasons why some people are more likely to be offered and to buy stolen goods, it is important to consider the relative influence of particular demographic and social variables. A statistical technique - logistic regression - was used to look at these factors in more depth. The analysis is conceptually quite straightforward. It involves building a mathematical model in which each variable makes a significant contribution to explaining the likelihood of buying stolen goods.[24] The model will not explain everything, however, because survey data inevitably fail to capture all the factors which affect offending behaviour (see Mayhew et al 1993).[25]

Those variables included in the model were lifestyle; wealth; age; gender; Acorn classification. Findings from this analysis are presented in Table 3.3.[26]

---

23 Weighted data. Unweighted N = 8753.
24 Those who self-reported buying stolen goods, as opposed to the wider category of 'risky buyers'. (A more detailed explanation of the B and R statistics are provided in Appendix 1).
25 Moreover, other important factors may have been omitted from the analysis, or may not have been collected in the survey. For example, the survey did not collect data on how the respondents knew or why they believed the goods they purchased really were stolen goods, whether they were bought from a friend or stranger - suspecting it might have been stolen - or from a known thief. This is because the stolen goods questions comprised only one, relatively small, section of the BCS. While it would have been useful for this study if the BCS questions had been more probing about how particular stolen goods were bought, this would have increased the cost and length of the survey considerably.
26 The full models and all relevant statistics are presented in Appendix 1 (Tables A1.1, A1.2 and A1.4).

Table 3.3 Buyers of Stolen Goods: Males and Females

Variable	s.s	odds ratio
Drugs problem in neighbourhood	**	1.3
Recent loss of wage earner in household	**	1.4
Not managing very well on income	***	1.5
ACORN GROUP †		
Rising/Striving	**	1.6
Expanding/Settling/Aspiring	*	1.5
Head of household self-employed[27]	*	1.4
Household without use of a car	*	1.3
Carried more than £200 of cash in		
the past month	**	1.5
Believe most burglaries in area		
committed by locals	**	1.3
High Risk Score	**	1.3
AGE ‡		
16 - 24	****	4.1
25 - 35	****	2.3
Being Male	****	1.6
No household contents insurance	*	1.3

s.s *p<0.05 **p<0.01 ***p<0.001 ****P<0.0001
Unweighted data. Source:1994 BCS. Follow-up A sample.[28]
† Estimate of the increased odds of buying stolen goods are compared with Acorn group: *Thriving*
‡ Estimate of the increased odds of buying stolen goods are compared with Age group 36-60

Of the 12 variables included in the model, age is the most powerful independent predictor of buying stolen goods. The odds of 16-24 year-olds buying stolen goods were more than four times those aged 36 to 60. The odds of 25 to 35 year-olds buying stolen goods were less than those in the younger age group, but more than twice those aged 36 to 60. Living in an area where people using and dealing in drugs is seen as a problem also slightly increased the odds of buying stolen goods (by a factor of 1.3). The odds of males buying stolen goods were more than one and a half times those of females.

The odds of those who regularly carry large sums of cash (£200 or more) of buying stolen goods were one and a half times those who did not do so. Stolen goods are invariably purchased with cash and thieves usually insist on immediate payment. It is possible that such large amounts of cash might be carried specifically for buying particular stolen goods, or simply to have money ready whenever such opportunities arise. Large sums of cash are also

---

27 Head of the household is or was self-employed the last time they worked.
28 Unlike the core sample, this sample included questions relating to 'stranger recognition' in the neighbourhood, household insurance and the largest sum of cash carried around in the last month - and was used because these were felt to be important variables. The sample was generated in the field at random and constitutes 50 percent of the main sample.

carried by those working in the informal economy or otherwise evading income tax and VAT, which may reflect a general willingness to commit or collude in crime.

To identify those with a lifestyle associated with a high risk of offending, a lifestyle risk score was generated from a number of responses to questions concerning drug use, going out behaviour and heavy drinking. One point was added to every respondent's risk score for each component of risky behaviour (see Appendix 1 for a more detailed explanation of how the scores were generated). Respondents with a high risk score were nearly one and a half times more likely to buy stolen goods than those with a medium or low risk score. Going out to certain pubs and clubs leads to a greater frequency of contact with people involved in crime. This will increase opportunities to buy stolen goods. Criminal peer groups are particularly likely to influence people who regularly drink heavily and take drugs (Cromwell and McElrath 1994; Graham and Bowling 1995:100).

Additional factors associated with buying stolen goods include 'Recent loss of wage earner in household', 'Household without use of a car', and 'Household without contents insurance'. These are most likely to be indicators of relative hardship and may represent elements of the complex matrix of interconnected factors which explain why some people buy stolen goods (Sutton 1995). Homes without contents insurance, for example, are most likely to be in areas suffering from high levels of burglary. Insurance premium levels are set on the basis of burglary risk, and because households with the highest burglary risks live in the poorest areas (see Hough 1984; Fattah 1993), poorer households experience disproportionately greater difficulty paying for insurance. In some of the highest risk areas, insurance cover may be refused outright. Sometimes locks, bolts and other security devices are a prerequisite of insurance cover, but householders may see these measures as too expensive.

Table 3.4 Whether household has contents insurance by those purchasing stolen goods

Household contents insured against theft	No	Yes
Bought stolen goods		
Yes %	20	11
n	153	367
No %	80	89
n	617	3148
Total	100	100

Follow-up sample A, weighted data, unweighted N

21

Table 3.4 shows that 20 percent of respondents without contents insurance against theft said they had bought stolen goods - compared with 11 percent who were insured. Logistic regression analysis reveals that this association seems to be independent of other factors which increase the likelihood of someone buying stolen goods, and that the odds of those without contents insurance buying stolen goods are increased by a factor of 1.3. The reasons for this, however, are unclear. An analysis of the association between different reasons given for not having insurance and buying stolen goods was inconclusive (See Table A1.3 Appendix 1). In most cases the numbers are too small to draw any reliable conclusions. Nevertheless, the association between non insurance and buying stolen goods probably reflects the higher insurance premiums demanded in the areas where these respondents live. People in these areas probably buy more stolen goods for a variety of reasons, including the opportunity to buy from the relatively larger number of thieves in their neighbourhood, the need to replace their own uninsured items if they are victims of theft, and buying in a neighbourhood where handling stolen goods is the norm (Hobbs 1989).

Living in an area where residents believed most burglaries are committed by locals increased the odds of buying stolen goods by a factor of 1.3. However, it should be noted that a respondent's own past burglary victimisation, or lack of it, was not significantly correlated with buying stolen goods.

One finding from this analysis which requires particular explanation is the association between living in a home where the respondent is self-employed, or the head of the household is self-employed, and buying stolen goods.[29] Although the BCS did not ask for further details about specific self-employed professions, a number of self-employed occupations such as market trader, scrap dealer, taxi-driver and small shop owner provide common outlets for stolen goods. Particular types of shop owners and other businessmen have been heavily implicated in fencing stolen goods for more than 150 years (see: Ferrier 1928; Gregory 1932; Benney 1936; Hall 1952; Munro 1972; Tobias 1974; Walsh 1977; Smithies 1984; Steffensmeier 1986; Parker et al 1988; Ward 1989; Foster 1990 and Tremblay et al 1994). This has not gone unnoticed and, in an attempt to reduce burglaries by making it harder to sell stolen jewellery, gold shops and jewellers were specifically targeted by the police as part of Operation Bumblebee, a particularly well publicised Metropolitan Police burglary reduction campaign. Particular jewellery shops in London were 'staked out' by Metropolitan police officers and suspected burglars arrested as they were about to enter and sell stolen property (Stockdale and Gresham 1995).

---

29   In 45 percent of the self-employed cases in this sample (weighted data) the respondent was head of the household.

Buying Stolen Goods: age and sex differences

The data presented so far considers buying stolen goods among all respondents, without differentiating between males and females or different age groups (other than in broad age bands). Gender is such a vital correlate of delinquency that it is important to establish the main explanatory variables associated with buying stolen goods for males and females separately. Tables 3.5 and 3.6 present the findings from this analysis, which includes a breakdown of age into six groups in order to compare with greater precision the association between age and buying stolen goods.

Table 3.5 Buying Stolen Goods: males

Variable	s.s	odds ratio
Drugs problem in neighbourhood	**	1.4
Not managing very well on income	****	1.9
ACORN GROUP †		
Rising/Striving	*	1.8
Expanding/Settling/Aspiring	*	1.8
Head of household self-employed[30]	*	1.7
Interviewers assessment of physical state of homes in neighbourhood as mainly bad or very bad ‡	*	2.2
Carried more than £200 of cash in the past month	**	1.5
AGE §		
16 - 17	****	5.1
18 - 21	****	7.0
22 - 25	****	4.7
26 - 30	****	2.5
31 - 36	***	2.0

s.s *p<0.05 **p<0.01 ***p<0.001 ****P<0.0001
Unweighted data. Source:1994 BCS. Follow-up A sample.[51]
† Estimate of the increased odds of buying stolen goods are compared with Acorn group: *Thriving*
‡ Estimate of the increased odds of buying stolen goods are compared with assessment of homes as mainly very good
§ Estimate of the increased odds of buying stolen goods are compared with age group 37-60.
A fuller version of this table is given in Appendix 1 (Table A1.5).

Comparing Table 3.5 with 3.6, age is clearly the most important variable for both sexes. The odds of males buying stolen goods are highest between 18 and 21 years. At this age the odds are seven times more than for males between 37 and 60 years. Thereafter, the odds of males buying stolen goods decrease with age.

---

30   Head of the household is or was self-employed the last time they worked.
31   Unlike the core sample, this sample included questions relating to 'stranger recognition' in the neighbourhood, household insurance and the largest sum of cash carried around in the last month - and was used because these were felt to be important variables. The sample was generated in the field at random and constitutes 50 percent of the main sample.

The odds of females buying stolen goods are highest between 22 and 25 years and are nearly five times greater than those aged between 37 and 60. The same odds apply to males of this age. Indeed, between 26 and 36 years, the odds of both females and males buying stolen goods are very similar - more than twice the odds for those aged between 37 and 60 years. After reaching 21 years of age, the odds of buying stolen goods are virtually the same for males and females.

Table 3.6 Buying Stolen Goods: females

Variable	s.s	*odds ratio*
Recent loss of wage earner in household	*	1.5
Not managing very well on income	*	1.4
Household without use of a car	***	1.8
Carried more than £200 of cash in		
the past month	*	1.5
Easy to recognise a stranger in neighbourhood	*	1.4
Believe most burglaries in area committed		
by locals	*	1.5
High Risk Score	**	1.6
AGE †		
16 - 17	**	3.8
18 - 21	***	2.5
22 - 25	****	4.7
26 - 30	****	2.8
31 - 36	***	2.1

s.s *p<0.05 **p<0.01 ***p<0.001 ****P<0.0001
Unweighted data. Source:1994 BCS. Follow-up A sample.[52]
† Estimate of the increased odds of buying stolen goods are compared with Age group 37-60
A fuller version of this table is given in Appendix 1 (Table A1.6).

In order to test the effect of age as well as gender, three separate models were fitted to the data for males in the broader age bands (16-24, 25-35 and 36-60). The same was done for females. The only statistically significant factor associated with buying stolen goods, for males between the age of 16 and 24, was living in an area where they believe people using or dealing in drugs is a 'big problem'. For females in this age range there were only two significant factors: not managing on their present income and carrying more than £200 of cash outside in the last month. Between the age of 25 and 35, there were only two significant findings for males: not managing on their income and believing that burglaries in their neighbourhood are committed by local residents. There were three significant factors for females in this age group: having a wage earner in the household who has lost their job; living in an inner city area and living in a household without the use of a car. Clearly, there are more factors not collected by the BCS which might be significantly associated with buying stolen goods among these younger age

---

32 Unlike the core sample, this sample included questions relating to 'stranger recognition' in the neighbourhood, household insurance and the largest sum of cash carried around in the last month - and was used because these were felt to be important variables. The sample was generated in the field at random and constitutes 50 percent of

groups - factors such as school exclusion, relationship with parents, delinquent peers, involvement in other offending and previous convictions.

The data were better suited to explaining why older respondents buy stolen goods. Turning to males between the age of 36 and 60, four significant factors remained in the model: losing a wage earner in the household, living in an area where the interviewer assessed the physical state of buildings as mainly bad or mainly very bad; having a total annual household income of less than £2,500 and not security marking their property against theft.[33] Females in this age group also had four significant factors: living in an area where people using or dealing in drugs is seen as a big problem; living in the poorest ACORN areas (rising or striving); having a high risk lifestyle and having a household income of less than £2,500.

Adverse factors and buying stolen goods

Moving on from the logistic regression models, the adverse area factors (ACORN category, drug problems and burglaries committed by locals) which were significantly correlated with buying stolen goods in the joint males and females model were also examined to see if respondents experiencing more than one of these factors were more likely to have bought stolen goods. The main aim here was to determine if the variables had a cumulative effect on buying stolen goods. In addition, adverse personal wealth indicators correlated with buying stolen goods (lost wage, not managing on income and not having contents insurance) were examined in the same way. Each of the three most important area problems and each of the three personal wealth indicators is counted as an adverse factor. The contribution of one or more adverse factors is then measured by way of a score ranging from zero to three (Tables 3.7 and 3.8).

Table 3.7 Adverse factors and buying stolen goods (area)

Number of adverse factors	Total Unweighted N			Bought Stolen goods %		
	Males	Females	ALL	Males	Females	ALL
0	553	612	1165	8	5	6
1	2110	2317	4427	14	8	10
2	1102	1434	2536	16	11	14
3	262	363	625	30	16	22

Follow-up sample A, weighted data

---

33   This is discussed further in relation to property marking recommendations in Chapter 8.

Table 3.8 Adverse factors and buying stolen goods (personal wealth)

Number of adverse factors	Total Unweighted N			Bought Stolen goods %		
	Males	Females	ALL	Males	Females	ALL
0	1800	1947	3747	11	6	8
1	1663	2089	3752	15	11	13
2	512	626	1138	22	12	17
3	52	64	116	40	18	28

Follow-up sample A, weighted data

This analysis shows that one in three males and one in seven females living in an area with three adverse factors admitted buying stolen goods (Table 3.7), compared with about one in 12 males and one in 20 females living in areas with none of these adverse factors. Similarly, four out of 10 males and almost two out of 10 females with three adverse personal wealth factors admitted buying stolen goods (Table 3.8) compared with about one in nine males and nearly one in 20 females with none of these adverse factors. Almost twice as many males with three adverse factors bought stolen goods as those with two adverse factors. This demonstrates a very clear cumulative, or 'marginal', effect of an increasing number of adverse factors. It may reflect the extent to which respondents experiencing more adverse factors - both where they live and in terms of their personal wealth - have a relatively smaller stake in society and therefore less to lose by breaking the law. However, many of these respondents may estimate the risk of getting caught as so minimal that the risk of losing anything is almost academic.

Summary and Conclusions

Buying stolen goods is significantly and independently correlated with being young and poor. People who fall into this category and buy stolen goods have relatively less to lose if they are caught breaking the law. As with most other crimes, young males are most likely to buy stolen goods. However, the effect of age on the odds of buying stolen goods is virtually the same for males and females after reaching 21 years. Disregarding age, lack of personal wealth remains closely associated with buying stolen goods - particularly among men. Cumulative adverse area and personal wealth factors also increase the percentage of females buying stolen goods, but to a lesser extent than males.

So far this study has looked at purchasing behaviour and self-reported offending from the BCS. For the first time, we have some indication of the demand for stolen goods at a national level. It is now time to begin looking in more depth at those who steal and deal in stolen goods.

4 A TYPOLOGY OF STOLEN GOODS MARKETS

Items stolen from householders and car owners are purchased by new owners to enjoy in their cars and their homes, but little has been written on the way this happens. Information used in this chapter was collected in order to understand more about the ways stolen goods pass to new owners. This information is needed to identify the different types of markets for stolen goods and will be particularly useful for informing future policing and crime prevention initiatives. The structure and organisation of five main markets for stolen goods are described. The roles of five of the sub-types of consumer and distributor, outlined in the previous chapter, are placed within each of these markets. Consumer III has no place in any of the markets for stolen goods since this type of thief simply keeps goods for their own use.

Types of market

There are five main types of market for stolen goods:

1 Commercial Fence Supplies

Goods are sold by thieves to fences with shops. *Distributors* such as small shopkeepers or jewellers are approached directly by thieves. Such sales are *private*. This type of market is maintained by the following buyers and sellers: *Distributor I; Distributor II and Distributor III.*

2 Commercial Sales

Goods are sold by the fence for a profit - either to the *consumer* or, more rarely, to another *distributor* who thinks they can sell again for additional profit. Customers buying in commercial sales are unlikely to know or believe that goods are stolen because *commercial fences* usually sell goods to innocent members of the public. Indeed, some *commercial fences* do not use criminal associates to sell - being able to use legitimate outlets such as their own retail or wholesale business. Sales are usually *open*, but can also be *private* if the customer believes the goods are stolen. Maintained by the following buyers and sellers: *Distributor I; Distributor II; Distributor III; Consumer I and Consumer II.*

3 Residential Fence Supplies

Distributors operating out of their own houses are approached directly by thieves or friends of thieves. All transactions are *private*. This type of market is maintained by the following buyers and sellers: *Distributor I; Distributor II and Distributor III.*

4 Network Sales

An initial friend (who may charge a small commission) is approached and the item for sale is shown or described. Word is then passed along friendship networks until a *consumer* is found. Sometimes goods are sold through the network with each new seller adding a little extra to the price. Network sales are usually *private*. Maintained by the following buyers and sellers: *Distributor I; Distributor II; Distributor III; Consumer I and Consumer II.*

5 Hawking

Thieves approach and sell directly to *consumers* who keep the stolen goods. Transactions in pubs and clubs are *semi-private*. Door-step sales are *private*. Maintained by the following buyers and sellers: *Distributor II; Distributor III; Consumer I and Consumer II.*

These are distinct categories, but they are not mutually exclusive because goods sold in one market may be sold on in another. For example, a thief may sell to a Commercial Fence who will then sell the goods to the public through commercial sales. Similarly, goods sold to a Residential Fence may well enter a Network Sales market.

The following pages describe each of the main markets for stolen goods in more detail and provide examples of buying and selling in them.[34]

---

34 This does not include how fences sell goods in *fencing markets* because it was extremely difficult to find any known fences who were prepared to be interviewed. Although one fence was identified through police contacts and was prepared to be interviewed at his business premises, the interview never took place because he was arrested for handling firearms and burglary and was awaiting trial throughout the interview stage of this research.

Commercial Fence Supplies

Most thefts are committed by thieves responding to what they know, or perceive, to be a general readiness to buy among members of the public. In this way markets for stolen goods are, indirectly at least, demand led. Commercial fences, because they operate out of business premises, provide a convenient, visible, and relatively safe place to sell stolen goods. They are always there and usually willing to buy.

Interviewees who had committed large numbers of burglaries, particularly of factories and shops where large amounts of valuable merchandise were removed, tended to rely upon one buyer to take certain types of goods off their hands. Thus, thieves in possession of stolen computer equipment, for example, would use a fence who specialised in computer sales. Similarly, stolen cigarettes would be sold to corner shops and alcohol to off-licences and pubs. Such fences were often found through criminal associates.

In the main, thieves did not talk of being recruited by a fence to steal for them. They were usually introduced to fences by other thieves who would vouch for their reliability. Otherwise, they had to 'recruit' a fence. Interviewees who sold stolen goods in this way tended to be more experienced thieves. They often targeted businessmen because they had to be accessible, clearly identifiable and obviously not off duty police officers.[35]

Transactions in commercial fence supplies markets

Approaching a businessman was considered by many thieves to be the quickest and most effective way to sell stolen goods. As one of the heroin users explained, it was better than walking up to a stranger on the street, because businessmen were seen as more likely to buy stolen goods and were more likely to carry the necessary cash:

> *I used to target businessmen a lot because they like business - no matter what kind of business it is. And they always had readily available money.*

One of the female heroin users, who had committed many burglaries, explained how small shopkeepers were approached:

> *You can go into your local shop where you go and buy your paper and milk, have a word with them in the back and be guaranteed, nine times out of ten, that he will buy it off you. They say they*

---

35   It is important to note that a study of 115 fences from North American police records (Walsh 1977) found that 48 percent were 'businessman-fences'.

want it for their own personal use, but I think they sell it on, because they know they are getting a bargain.

Another heroin user said she always targeted small businessmen, even if she had never sold to them before. Others said that shopkeepers were lower down their list of preferred buyers, but that if they were in a hurry for money or felt that it was too risky to be in possession of the stolen goods, they would go to a shopkeeper.

More usually thieves went to shopkeepers they had dealt with before, or those with a reputation for buying. One adult burglar[36] explained his first encounter with a shop owner who then regularly bought stolen goods from him:

What I did I went up to the youngest bloke in there. There was like an old bloke and a woman on the till. So I've explained that I live across the road and that I've got a big box of fags and that I don't need them and I want to sell them. And he's said: "Where do you live" and he's said "Right I'll let you know." The next thing you know the old bloke's come along with his son at half past six and knocked on the door. He said: "Where are these fags then?" I said: "They're upstairs". He's said: "Bring them over to that gate then." [by the side of his shop] So I took them over and he said: "What do you want for these, and what do you want for these?"

After this episode the burglar sold stolen electrical goods to the same shop owner. Although he always received more money from a residential fence whom he preferred to deal with, circumstances and convenience sometimes dictated that he sold to the shopkeeper instead:

Sometimes we had too much, or it was too great a distance, or we were in a hurry for the money - sometimes it's just desperateness. Or we didn't feel we had enough to take over there... [To a drug dealing residential fence].[37]

A young burglar explained how he first made contact with his commercial fence and how their relationship developed:

One of our men we got him in the Yellow Pages. He was a proper authorised Apple [computer] dealer - like we used to sell him the quads[38] at say what come to four grand or something [£4,000 retail price] - we'd sell it to him for two. Half price. And then he'd

---

36   The term 'burglars', as used in this report, is not necessarily self-definitive (See Wright and Decker 1994).
37   This fence preferred to buy in bulk so as to limit the number of transactions he had to make with thieves.
38   Specialist computers costing between £4,000 and £18,000.

*just do a few things with it and put it up for sale for the full price.
My mate phoned him up - it was by chance really - lucky really. He's
said "I've got this to sell" and he's [the dealer] gone: "Well I'll come
down and have a look." And when he come down and seen it he
must have thought: 'well it's definitely funny', y'know what I mean
- we're just like young people, we're not like office bods really are
we. So then, when he's bought that, he's gone: "Yeh phone me any
time." So then it just went on.*

*Some of the people that he was selling the goods to, he was giving
us the addresses after. He's gone: "Get me that." And we'd go and
have 'em. Obviously he's got the legit people he sells to, and the
dodgy people he sells to. He wouldn't set up the dodgy people but
others - he might give us their address. Like shops, garages - lock-
ups. The geezer he's put us onto bought six or seven quads. He
wouldn't send us 'round for just one quad it would have to be a
parcel of 'em, like a lump of 'em, and we would do it like that. He'd
give us a price in advance and obviously we had to give him a
discount 'cause he put us on to it.*

The fence asked these young burglars to steal for him on six occasions and
each time they were successful in stealing back items he had supplied to
legitimate customers. The fence was never arrested and the burglars were
never charged with stealing computer equipment. There is no way of telling
from this research how widespread such practices are. However, another
interviewee talked about a similar relationship he had with the owner of a
specialist car stereo business, where he would be directed to cars that had
just had expensive stereos installed. He stole the stereos and sold them back
to the dealer, who then, on at least two occasions, installed improved
security systems and a replacement stereo system in the victim's car. Other
research (Cromwell et al 1991) has found evidence that tradesmen sell
information about the contents and security of customer's houses to
burglars, or returned and did burglaries themselves. Wright and Decker
(1994) found several burglars who had jobs that gave them a chance to enter
other people's homes to look for potential victims.

Most burglars and thieves did not feel that it was risky selling stolen property
to shops that bought second-hand goods. However, those who were
frequently consuming illegal drugs, such as heroin and cocaine, tended to
steal more often than others. They often stole on a daily basis and so had to
find other buyers to avoid over-supplying their regular customers.

Sellers visit business premises which they can leave quickly to avoid
detection if the shopkeeper reports them to the police. It is also easier to
avoid detection if the buyer is subsequently arrested, because he is unlikely

to be able to provide the police with any details about the thieves he has been buying from. However, dealing with 'unknown' shops can be a source of anxiety for thieves. One interviewee who had been involved in 20 street robberies and had sold the jewellery he acquired to different shops on each occasion, remained anxious about having to give his name and address and an explanation for why he was selling. Another interviewee described how he had accompanied a friend to a camera exchange shop to sell a camcorder they had stolen from a car. The staff had asked his friend: "Where he got it" and "how long he had it" and "what kind of batteries did it take" and "did he have a receipt." However, despite this cross examination, his friend successfully sold the camera in the shop for £150.

Very little is known about how frequently, and to what extent, proprietors and employees of second-hand shops, corner shops, pawn brokers, jewellery shops and scrap yards genuinely seek to establish that they are buying legitimate and not stolen goods. Many of the interviewees in this study felt that the were asked set, or 'pat', questions more for the shopkeeper's own protection from prosecution than from any desire to establish whether the goods were stolen or not. When they sold goods to these businesses, all the interviewees thought that the shopkeepers knew for sure that they were stolen but that they required a story from them which they felt obliged to provide. As one burglar explained:

> *I sussed it in the end when I was in London later on. I know they all do it now - you can tell by the way they say it. You just go in and say "Oh excuse me do you buy scrap gold and anything else?" And he'll turn around and say: "Oh what have you got then?" And like he'll probably not look up at yer and he'd say: "All yours then is it?" and at the same time be almost shifting it away. So then like, getting ready to take it. So you know then he's not going to be giving you it back. Or straightaway he'll say: "How much do you want?" He'd say: "You have got a bit of ID on you haven't you?" - almost casual. It's the attitude they give out. It's quite easy to spot it now. But at first when they started asking questions I was getting paranoid and going. But you can go to another jeweller and he'll say: "What are you selling then?" and straightaway he'd say: "No! no! no!" because he knows it's been stolen because you wouldn't be selling it at such a cheap price. Or he'd say: "Can you prove where you got this from?" If they say that, then you're stuffed.[39]*

One of the YLS respondents explained how, when he first became involved in stealing as a teenager, he regularly sold stolen goods to second-hand shops:

---

39   See also Stone 1975.

We used to sell to second-hand shops but they knew [the goods were stolen]. I mean one day we used to go in there with a bike and the next day go in with a stereo - and they didn't know? We never got friendly with them. All it was to us was money. They knew where it was coming from. All you had to do was like sign this thing to say it was yours so it like covers them doesn't it.

Despite widely held beliefs that businessmen are likely to be dishonest, thieves still employed protective strategies to reduce risks when selling to new businesses. Where thieves did not have 'special' relationships with a commercial fence it was necessary to interpret the potential buyer's 'attitude' to determine if they could be 'trusted'.

Having a system where sellers must sign a record book to say that goods offered for sale are their own and record their address provides the commercial fence with grounds to demonstrate he, or she, did not know or believe that the goods were stolen. The thief can easily lie about ownership and these same lies protect the shopkeeper from suspicion. Even where proof of address is required, a burglar can easily supply a stolen driving licence or household bills. Such record books may actually facilitate selling stolen goods by reducing the fear of arrest among shopkeepers. The onus should be placed on the shopkeeper to require a higher degree of proof of ownership such as a receipt, the original packaging that the goods were supplied with, receipts for repairs, or perhaps even a document supplied by the police to say that expensive goods offered for sale have not been reported stolen. A national computerised database would be required for this to be effective.

None of the interviewees described these fences as 'professional' handlers of stolen goods. Rather they were portrayed as businessmen who bought stolen goods when the opportunity arose to make a profit from buying at a bargain price (see also Chambliss 1984: 50). These markets could be tackled by reducing such opportunities and increasing the risks and effort involved. Chapter 8 discusses in more detail how this might be achieved.

The BCS revealed that respondents in households where the head of the household was self-employed were significantly more likely to have bought stolen goods. This can be at least partly explained by the greater number of offers that the self-employed receive. One respondent, for example, had recently set up a small car repair business and described how such offers occur:

It was stolen vehicles this morning - I was putting a car on one of the trailers - a stock car - and this bloke said I can get you a bit of this or a bit of that. I don't know him - I've only been there two weeks. He was offering cars and stolen MOTs. I'll always get offered stolen goods because of who I am.

Once word gets around that a certain shopkeeper, businessman or other commercial fence will buy stolen goods then they are likely to be flooded with offers to buy and may be reluctant to refuse for fear of being given away to the police (see Maguire's account of a shopkeeper's experience in Appendix 3). One solution to this problem is for the fence to limit the number of suppliers by offering less money than before in the hope that thieves will try selling elsewhere. Although it is not known whether this is a strategy that fences intentionally adopt (it could just as easily be explained as greed), several respondents said that they stopped going to shopkeepers and other fences because "…they started paying rubbish money".

The successful fence not only has to limit the number of suppliers but must also keep trade secrets from them. Most of those interviewed said that once they had sold to a fence they knew little or nothing about where or to whom the goods were next sold. 'Distancing' between fences and thieves appears to be the general rule.[40]

To minimise risks from legitimate customers observing illegal transactions, criminal entrepreneurs seek to keep dealings with thieves separate from the rest of the enterprise. Reuter (1985) has described how this happens in other illegal markets. Thieves who regularly sold stolen jewellery to a jewel fence were taken to a separate room away from customers. Those who sold stolen cars or motorbikes to vehicle breakers' yards were usually instructed to strip the vehicle of components and remove serial numbers themselves - presumably so that regular 'respectable' employees were not 'contaminated', so that the commercial fences did not have to do the work themselves and to protect them from incrimination. Keeping employees 'clean' is important in maintaining a 'front of legitimacy'. Shopkeepers who bought stolen goods sometimes asked for them to be taken to a back door or left in an unlocked car boot. More cautious fences met in car parks, fields, woods, on wasteland or other neutral, but safe, locations.

Commercial Sales

Commercial fences operate from businesses and so they can pass brand new goods on to consumers who may not be aware that the goods are stolen (Sutton 1995). Corner shops and market traders were regularly referred to as outlets for items that had been stolen from shops or warehouses. Stolen gold, for example, is cut up and melted down and can be made into new

---

40   There are exceptions: two interviewees said their fences provided them with a customer's address so that goods could be stolen back.

jewellery. Similarly, jewels can be placed into new settings and sold to innocent consumers (Wright and Decker 1994). Commercial fences also sell 'used' stolen goods through their own second-hand shops (Parker et al 1988).

A commercial fence has somewhere to store the goods, can transport them and has access to an existing customer base. This means he or she can demand higher prices than residential fences and hawkers because they need not be in such a hurry to sell. Commercial sales are often well organised, but the fence faces significant risks, particularly if thieves are not kept separate from the main business. However, the risks tend to be outweighed by the huge profits which can be made in the short term.

Transactions in commercial sales markets

Many consumers in commercial sales markets pay the full retail price for new goods, unaware that they have bought stolen goods. Similarly, those who buy from second-hand shops and markets may be innocent buyers because of the very openness of the transaction and the accepted legitimacy of the outlet.

Buying in commercial sales markets carries relatively little risk, even for those who know or believe they are buying stolen goods from a commercial fence. This is because in most cases the fence 'sanitises' stolen goods by buying and selling them through his or her legitimate business. Whoever buys them next receives a receipt which serves to 'legitimise' the purchase (Klockars 1974).

Residential Fence Supplies

Residential fences usually operate out of their own homes. Some residential fences were described as being relatively well off with mortgages and families. Like commercial fences, they are careful to limit the number of suppliers they have dealings with in order to keep the supply under control. Some thieves could not deal directly with a particular fence but had to go through friends or accomplices. They often required an introduction by 'trusted' criminal associates. Residential fences may be drug dealers or former thieves who have 'crime-switched' to less risky offending.

Some fences were also burglars taking advantage of buying opportunities. One interviewee, for example, had acted as a residential fence when the chance arose. He bought his partner's share of stolen clothes from a ram raid on a shop because he had successfully sold his own share, while his friend had been unable to find a suitable buyer. He then sold the clothes for a profit from his sister's flat. Others bought items of stolen jewellery and VCRs from other thieves if they thought they could sell them for more money. Some had switched from thieving on realising the reduced risk and potentially greater profitability associated with buying and selling stolen goods. A young car radio thief, for example, stopped stealing and switched to selling stereos, stolen by his friends, because it was less risky and more profitable.

Transactions in residential fence supplies

In several cases, thieves sold only to relatives, friends, or relatives of friends who were residential fences (see also Wright and Decker 1994). This 'keeping it in the family' approach serves to minimise the risk for fence and thief alike. Goods were usually sold to residential fences at their homes or in safe neutral locations. One of the heroin users explained how he would go about selling goods to his fence:

> Park the car with the goods down in the car park, walk up, knock him. He would come down to the car and we will pull into the garage or whatever and sort through everything. Most of them won't let the things be brought to the house because you tend to find a lot tend to be older with family and they [the family] don't really realise what is going on …so his wife doesn't know they've got a garage outside loaded up with about 16 videos and he does very well out of it.

Car stereos are frequently sold through residential fences. However, local markets for car stereos can approach saturation point. When this happens selling becomes more difficult and even unattractive:

> …I mean once you've serviced everyone on the estate, y'know eight or nine people, that was it then. That would be the only time I would deal with them, I'd rather deal with the middleman.

Business owners were also mentioned as people who have the money to buy stolen car stereos and many friends and relatives who are in the market for a 'bargain'. It is important to point out, however, that such buyers should be distinguished from commercial fences because they do not use their business as a 'front' for selling stolen goods. A 19-year-old offender, serving his second sentence in a YOI for burglary, described how he regularly sold stolen car stereos to factory owners during the day - and how he believed these residential fences, in turn, sold them on from their homes:

> My cassettes [car stereo systems] go to Turkish factories. You know a Turkish factory that makes clothes and all that. You see my Dad's Turkish and I know a lot of Turkish people who own these factories

and that and I go to them and sell these radios to them for top money. And they will put them in their car or sell them to their cousins and uncles and their family or they will ship them back over to Cyprus.

The way residential fences operate can be distinguished from commercial fencing transactions by the fact that they do not sell to consumers through respectable business outlets and rarely deal with strangers. Sometimes they do not pay for goods immediately, but sell for thieves on a commission basis. Some thieves said that their residential fence would only buy in bulk so as to avoid large numbers of petty transactions.

Although they can sell directly to consumers, residential fences are probably not as remote from other criminal networks as most commercial fences, who only sell directly to consumers. Indeed, residential fences frequently use Network sales markets to distribute stolen goods.

Network sales

Network sales markets comprise loosely connected groups of friends, neighbours, colleagues and workmates. Sales among close friendship and family networks nearly always take place in the privacy of people's homes, privately at the workplace, or at pre-arranged locations. Orders for specific types of stolen goods are sometimes met through network sales, or goods are bought and sold along a network until one of the buyers becomes the final consumer. Although residential fences may sometimes utilise network sales markets to sell stolen goods, not everyone making money through buying and selling in network sales is a residential fence. In a previously unpublished account of a fencing operation in the 1980s (see Appendix 3) Maguire and Webster describe how the owner of a general store became a residential fence[41] and how a stolen television set was sold on through a network of nine handlers with each making a small profit.

The residential fence, like the commercial fence, buys directly from thieves. And because thieves know where to find them, residential fences are more frequently involved in buying and selling than the occasional 'opportunistic' participants in network sales.

The BCS respondents who bought at least one of the eight most commonly stolen consumer durables yet another way (9 percent) were likely to have bought them through network sales, since such expensive items are rarely hawked door-to-door. These sales take place in what is likely to be one of the most difficult markets to police.

---

41   As the stolen goods were not sold out of the shop he was not operating as a commercial fence.

Transactions in network sales

In general, participants in network sales only sell to people they know and sometimes the final consumer is only one or two links in the chain away from a fence. A 20-year-old female explained how she occasionally used network sales to distribute goods that lorry drivers were pilfering and selling to her self-employed husband:

> We got a lot of crystal - glasses, decanters, tumblers, sherry glasses, champagne glasses. Again, from a delivery man. Somehow it worked out that there was an extra crate of Edinburgh Crystal on the lorry. So the girls at work said: "Wooh crystal...!" I went into the office and said: "You'll never guess what he's got now, he's got crystal." And all their eyes like lit up and they said: "How much does he want for that?" They just said: "Well bring 'em in and we'll choose." Six glasses of this and six glasses of that. There was a lot. And that did worry me because I didn't want all that in my car in case I got pulled.[42] We used to joke about it and they'd say: "Well what have you got this week then...?"

One theme that emerged from the interviews was the way that people acquiring stolen goods sparked off a desire among their friends to obtain a similar bargain. As one of the adult prisoners explained, this often meant that a demand for more of the same would travel back down the chain of buyers and sellers to the original thief:

> It sort of went in phases. Some months, for quite a few months, it would be car stereos that everyone was getting. And then it would be videos. And then it would be clothes. You see, with it being a council estate, like - if one person has got a cassette and he's told his friend, or who he works with, then he tells his friend, and he wants one. And then he tells another friend, and he wants one. 'Cause they're so cheap everybody wants one.

A male heroin user explained in more detail the role of residential fences within network sales:

> They have their network of people. They know people, then people know other people, it's only word of mouth. Say if you wanted a leather jacket and I sold you a leather jacket, you knew full well it's stolen. If you're out one night and a couple of your friends go: "That's a lovely jacket where did you get that?" You go: "Oh, so and so got it for me, I can get you one." You've got your central dealer and two or four people who they are close to. From them four

---

people, you've probably got another six to eight who they sell to on
a regular basis. From that six to eight, there are probably another
18 to 20 who buy every now and then.

Hence, demand of this kind comes either directly to the thief via friendship
networks or through residential fences.

Very expensive car stereos are often sold through networks of many friends
with each making a little profit as they sell it on. A 31-year-old offender, with
a considerable history of car crime (having recently completed four years of
imprisonment for car theft), explained how residential fences could supply
their customers with the exact car stereos they wanted through network
sales markets:

If you want a particular stereo it might take two days but you'll get
one. A few phone calls and that would be it. You ring one person.
He might ring three or four to see if they've got one and they'll ring
about three or four to see if they've got one. It's like at the end of
the day you've got about 50 people from one phone call. You can
get anything…anything.

When stereos are not supplied to order in this way, the person who finally
buys and actually uses the stereo, bought in a network sales market, is likely
to be the one who is most passionate about owning it:

Because we were talking about stereos and swapping a few stereo
bits, he says: "I've got an Alpine if you know anybody wants one."
And I made a deal with him. I looked at it, I said: "I'll have to have
a look at that, I've never had an Alpine before." I thought: "I'm
having that." He said: "I don't really want to sell it, but seeing as I
know your Dad you can have it for 100 pounds." And I stood him
[paid a deposit] at 80 pounds.

One of the YLS respondents worked as a transport manager for a large
manufacturer. He had always worked and had on several occasions boosted
his income through selling brand new stolen goods. He describes how, a
year before the interview, he sold stolen compact disks bought from a friend
(a residential fence), who, in turn, had bought them from the original thief:

The box cost a hundred quid. I knew I could sell 'em for four quid a
piece. It took a week and a half to sell all 200. I went into a pub
and started putting the word about that I've got some pop-chart
cds, all mixed. The thing is when you're selling 'em for three or four
quid a piece people don't particularly go for one - they come up
and buy, probably, 10 or 12. If I got a phone call they would say:

Figure 4.1

	DISTRIBUTOR			CONSUMER			TYPE		
	I	II	III	I	II	III	Private	Semi-private	Open
Commercial Fence Supplies	✓	✓	✓				✓		
Residential Fence Supplies	✓	✓	✓				✓		
Network Sales	✓	✓	✓	✓	✓		✓		
Commercial Sales	✓	✓	✓	✓	✓		✓		✓
Hawking		✓	✓	✓	✓		✓	✓	

"Can you meet us up so and so, I've got three or four people that would like to buy some cds." So I'd just shoot off in the car.

Roughly, I made about 600 quid. The thing is, you can't afford to go in and buy five or six boxes because you flood your own market. Because I only know so many people. It's like a chain letter - you can only go so far. It's just when somebody comes up with something that I think I can get rid of. Now, because I've got the money, I don't bother... it's only if something really good comes up - I'll have a go at it.

Hawking markets

These can be found in certain establishments such as clubs, pubs or cafes, where thieves usually sell directly to strangers. They are also found in neighbourhoods where thieves sell stolen goods door-to-door - sometimes to strangers but also to people they know are likely to buy. Those who frequently use heroin are more prepared to take risks and sell goods around the neighbourhood - 'cold calling' when necessary - and are generally less concerned about getting a fair price.

Transactions in hawking markets

Hawkers were described as people who did not have a fence. Despite the absence of a middleman, they were generally seen as making less money from their transactions with consumers. One of the adult burglars interviewed in prison had been a heavy user of heroin. He also made money through shoplifting and would sell stolen jeans and other clothing on a door-to-door basis around Manchester. When asked about how much money he could make, he replied: "I never thought of it that way, the only thing I had on me mind was drugs." Although he said he was never reported to the police while doing this, hawking stolen goods in this way was more difficult for those known to the police. As one female drug dealer said:

You can't afford to be walking around the streets once you're known 'cause you'll get pulled y'know. Sometimes you can get a taxi like or you'll bring a person to your house.

During an interview with a young male respondent from the YLS sample, the interview was interrupted when he answered a knock at the door to buy stolen cigarettes for himself and his mother from a hawker. This particular hawker was described by the interviewee as: "a smack-head[43] in a taxi." He went on to explain:

---

43   Heroin addict.

The smack-heads they come round and they offer things at cheap prices. They come round with bags knocking on doors. People know their faces anyway because they see them walking about and that, and they just come to your door and that. Just knock on and ask if you're interested in buying. You get tellies and videos floating about but you get mostly stuff from shops. Mostly, like household stuff like deodorants. Most people buy the deodorants because it's cheap. And shampoo. You get coffee, bacon and stuff...

Many of those who were interviewed had frequently, even daily, been offered stolen goods, usually clothes, by people calling at their home. Those who bought them were aware that the seller was vulnerable, sometimes desperate, and would often reduce their prices.

Stealing to order

Stealing to order takes place within four out of the five stolen goods markets described - the exception being hawking markets. Stealing to order may happen when a consumer approaches a fence - who then approaches a thief directly. Alternatively, the consumer may approach a thief. In addition, a fence may place 'standing orders' with thieves for goods that are in general demand. Goods most commonly stolen appear to be those which can be located through inside knowledge or observation e.g.: state-of-the-art car stereos, computer/office equipment, motor vehicles and their components.

Goods which are stolen to order are typically those in short supply in illicit markets, yet highly desirable - items such as camcorders, state-of-the-art electrical goods, computers and computer chips, fast-moving consumer goods like cigarettes and expensive meat, and essential goods such as baby clothes.

Domestic burglars are least likely to be motivated by requests to steal to order, probably because it is difficult to know in advance whether any particular dwelling contains the items requested. Stealing to order is most commonly carried out by shoplifters who steal items of clothing of a particular type and size, or even food items on a consumer's shopping list. Thieves stealing to order are often highly motivated. To meet an order they sometimes undertake extensive forays until items are located.

In some cases, the thief did not know how to steal the items that had been requested:

"I've been asked to steal a couple of mobile phones, but I don't know how to get them."

42

In others, it was just not possible to steal what people wanted:

> *"It wasn't always easy, a lot of times we'd try and try and try and there was just no way we could do it."*

The degree of effort described by offenders stealing to order was a recurring theme, particularly among those who stole car stereos. Expensive car stereos are desirable, easy to sell and, once located, easy to steal. In some cases stealing to order plainly resulted in an increase in offending:

> *One particular person wanted video cassettes. He just wanted as many as we could get. He wanted the good ones. And of course we'd go in and just spend the whole day just going into the same shop and out. I remember in [name of shop in name of town] they were doing them on special offer in packs of four. So we were going for them as often as we could. We did it solidly for a couple of days and then over a week or so we still went in and got a couple of bags, so I reckon we must have got about 100 to 150 tapes.*

To emphasise the degree of motivation among thieves who steal to order, the following example is taken from an interview with a 25-year-old male. He had recently served 16 months in prison for handling a stolen car, driving whilst disqualified and possession of cocaine. He was stealing a car stereo to order following a direct request from a consumer:

> *At the age of 15 we used to sort of hang around in the park, mostly the same age, a few older. People would stop in their cars and say "Oh can you get me this?" Well, obviously, you like to get as much as you can so you'd say like you want so much for it and you'd come to some arrangement. Sometimes you'd say, like, I want 100 pounds and they'd say - yeah fine. Sometimes they'd say that would be too much. Then we'd go out and look in every car park.*

When expensive car stereos are stolen to order like this, the price is negotiated in advance. From the moment a price has been agreed the particular type of stereo then represents hard cash, and even car alarms are not always a deterrent (see also Wright and Decker 1994). Another offender described how he went looking for a Kenwood stereo with his cousin after someone had offered to pay them £70 for one. They set off at 4pm and found one at 8pm. The car, on the driveway of a house, was alarmed but they knew that the alarm on that model of car would only be triggered by opening the car door. So they broke the side window with a screwdriver and climbed inside. They sold the stereo that same night.

A 25-year-old secretary, mentioned earlier for her involvement in network

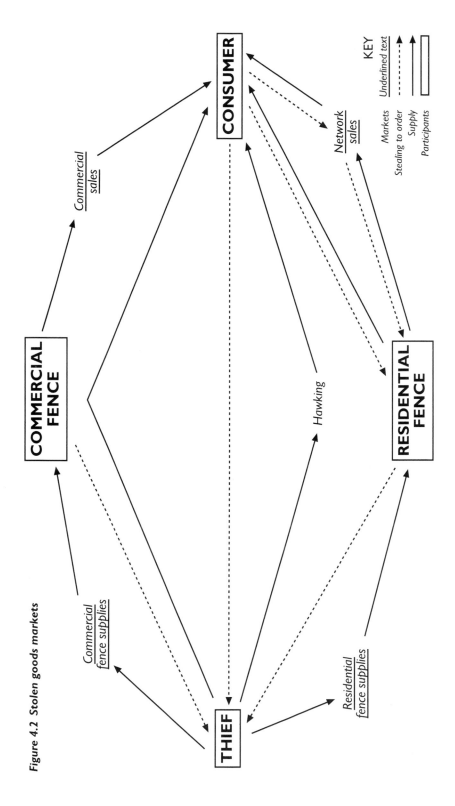

Figure 4.2 Stolen goods markets

sales, had also bought such goods as a stolen television and a stolen VCR. She explained how telling her boyfriend that she wanted an up-to-date hi-fi system resulted in them paying a visit to a well known residential fence:

I hadn't got a hi-fi and I wanted one of those little midi-systems. You know just with the cd and the tape. I didn't want a big turntable, and my boy friend's brother-in-law could get hold of them. Where he got them from I don't know, but he said: "If I can get you one would you be interested?" I said: "Well for the right money yeah." I said to my boy friend: "I'd love one of those midi-systems." He said: "Well don't pay full price for it, I'll see if [x] can get you one."

So he took me 'round to [x's] and he knows all the right people, or all the wrong people, and he says: "Yeah what do you want?" And I said: "Well I want a little diddy one, with a tape and a cd." And I said: "I don't want a turntable and I don't want to pay a lot for it." He said: "About a hundred and fifty pounds?" I said: "If you can get one for that, that's fine." But I didn't know what make, so I said to him: "If you get it and I don't like it, I'm not having it." He said: "That's all right, I'll get rid of it." He told me he was going down [name of retail store] to get it.

When he came up with the goods and said: "There's your thing, I got it in [name of retail store]." I said: "What do you mean you got it in [retail store]?" He said it actually came off the display shelf. He said: "Not me personally, but a friend did." I was gobsmacked. I thought: Ooh gawd." I said: "Oh no what if they catch up with you." Then I started to panic. He said: "Oh you can have it for a hundred [pounds]." [44]

The fence was arrested shortly after this episode and his arrest and involvement with thieves was given quite a lot of coverage in the local press. As a result, the hi-fi was hidden in the interviewee's loft. She was so afraid that the police would learn that she had bought it, and that she would lose her job, she said she would never buy anything stolen again.

Summary and Conclusions

The typology of stolen goods markets, outlined in this chapter, provides a framework for structuring, and thus better understanding, transactions in

---

[44]   The retail price was said to be £400. She was able to buy it for such a low price because the fence was her boyfriend's brother-in-law. See Chapter 5 for usual prices.

illegal merchandise. It explains where markets are likely to be, what they are like, and who will be dealing in them.

This chapter also described how on some occasions, particularly in network sales, thieves steal to order. It has touched upon the way thieves selling in hawking markets target particular neighbourhoods to sell stolen goods and the way neighbourhood networks create demand for stolen goods and thereby increase levels of ownership of stolen goods in certain areas.

In both network sales and commercial fence supplies markets, sellers are often aware of the need to control the level of demand for their stolen goods by restricting supply. They do this by using more than one buyer. In this way, the price they get for stolen goods is commensurate with the risks associated with stealing and/or selling. There are many policy implications arising from these findings, which are considered in Chapters 8 and 9.

It is surprising that so many thieves thought small shopkeepers and other business owners were characteristically dishonest. Business owners who buy stolen goods were seen as condoning theft and this in turn appears to reinforce opinions among offenders that 'legitimate' business and crime are in many ways the same thing. There may be scope for undermining this belief and creating a perception of increased risk associated with selling stolen goods to 'unknown' businessmen. Chapters 8 and 9 detail possible ways of achieving this.

5 HOW STOLEN GOODS MARKETS OPERATE

This chapter focuses on the nature of transactions in stolen goods and examines some of the operational concerns of those involved in stolen goods markets. Areas covered include aspects of the (non-contractual) relationship between offer and acceptance, transportation, entrepreneurs, careers, elasticity of demand, prices and sales.

Stolen goods markets share many of the characteristics of legitimate markets. Certainly, many of the concerns of those involved in stealing or dealing in stolen goods appear quite similar to those of legitimate businesspeople. The markets are characterised by entrepreneurs and others, including family groups, who work according to the same principles which govern legitimate markets, such as warehousing, marketing and risk taking. There are suppliers and dealers - who may be residential or commercial fences. Sometimes stolen goods are stored, while at other times turnover is very quick. And they often need some form of transportation.

Offer and acceptance in stolen goods markets

The effect of offers on people's willingness to buy stolen goods is particularly important for the way stolen goods markets operate. If consumers do not seek out stolen goods, then accepting offers is the only other way they can knowingly buy them. For handlers of stolen goods, this is fundamentally linked with the concept of crime as opportunity (Mayhew et al 1976).

The authors of a North American self-report study (Cromwell and McElrath 1994) were unable to find a direct relationship between several demographic variables (age, sex, ethnicity and income) and the purchase of stolen goods. Instead, they found that those with criminal *motivation* 'would buy stolen goods if offered' and those given the *opportunity*, 'being offered stolen goods', were more likely to say they bought them. This assumes a typical scenario in which sellers approach people they do not know and make them completely unsolicited offers out of the blue. While the authors claim that opportunity to purchase stolen goods is a major factor in explaining why people buy such goods, this conclusion is flawed on three counts. As the authors admit, it is possible that having a **real** opportunity to buy stolen goods increases the likelihood that someone will say they **would** buy them (so called *motivation* to buy). But, it also seems reasonable to suggest that those who bought stolen goods were more likely to say they would buy stolen goods if they had the chance.[45] More importantly, there is no way of knowing if *offers* to buy stolen goods result from past buying behaviour or stem from buyers letting it be known in the neighbourhood, or elsewhere, that they are 'in the market' for particular products.

The BCS data was examined to look in more depth at the relationship between offers and buying stolen goods. Respondents were asked about the number of offers of stolen goods they received. The majority said they were not offered stolen goods in the past year **and** had never bought stolen goods over a five-year period (82 percent). The remaining 18 percent (1573) had either been offered stolen goods, bought stolen goods, or both.

Table 5.1 Offered stolen goods in past 12 months

	%	Unweighted N
Never	89	7771
Once	4	332
Few times	6	518
Often	1	127
Don't know/Refused	<1	5
Unweighted N	100	8753

Weighted percentages. Source 1994 BCS.

Table 5.1 shows that a total of 11 percent had been offered stolen goods in the past year. There is no way of distinguishing between offers explicitly invited, offers occurring due to past buying behaviour, and unexpected offers received by respondents who had no prior intention to buy. It should be noted, however, that being offered stolen goods will, in many cases, be intrinsically linked to either past or present buying behaviour.

The BCS did not ask whether offers of stolen goods were accepted. However, this can be gauged to some extent by looking at those offered stolen goods in the past year who never bought any in the past five years. These are defined as Decliners in the following table.

---

45   These criticisms stem from the fact that there was no measure of time-order in the data.

Table 5.2 Level of involvement with stolen goods by age group and sex

		Men			Women		
		16-24	25-35	36-59	16-24	25-35	36-59
Offered	%	**39**	16	7	**18**	7	3
	N	(234)	(217)	(164)	(145)	(138)	(79)
Decliners	%	46	54	**73**	50	62	**72**
	N	(112)	(118)	(120)	(351)	(253)	(266)

Unweighted N. Weighted percentages. The percentage of decliners in the above table is based on those who were offered stolen goods.

The relationship between offers and buying behaviour was examined to see whether being offered stolen goods influenced buying behaviour. Only seven percent of those who admitted buying stolen goods in the past five years said they had **not** been offered stolen goods in the last 12 months. There is a clear association between age, gender and being offered or buying stolen goods (Table 5.2). A greater proportion of those aged between 16 and 24 were offered stolen goods. Males were offered more, and more males bought stolen goods than females. Almost half of males aged 16 to 24 had been offered or bought stolen goods. More than twice as many males are offered stolen goods as females and nearly twice as many bought them.

It is particularly interesting to note that a higher proportion of females up to the age of 35 declined to buy. However, once in their mid thirties, there is virtually no difference between males and females declining to buy.

Multivariate analysis of offers

As with buying stolen goods (Chapter 3), the BCS variables that were thought (on the basis of existing knowledge) most likely to be correlated with being offered stolen goods were analysed. Over 30 variables were examined including: lifestyle; wealth; age; gender; Acorn classification and previous victimisation[46] (see Table 5.3).

The odds of males being offered stolen goods was twice that for females. The odds of 16-24-year-olds being offered stolen goods was six times greater than for those in the 36-60 age group, and twice as great as for 25-35-year-olds. The odds of people being offered stolen goods who said they believed that many of their neighbours had stolen goods in their homes[47] was more than twice the odds of those who thought 'none' or 'not very many neighbours' owned stolen goods.

---

46   Tested for entry into the model using the forward stepwise method (Norusis, 1990, p131). See Appendix 1. The full list of variables tested for entry into the model can be found in Appendix 1.

47   The variable used was generated from a combination of those who said that either 'a lot' or 'quite a few' of their neighbours had stolen goods such as televisions and VCRs in their homes.

Personally knowing someone who had been burgled in the past year nearly doubled the odds of receiving an offer to buy stolen goods. This may reflect where respondents live because acquisitive crimes, such as burglary, are not evenly distributed (Trickett et al 1995) and burglars frequently steal and sell goods locally[48] (see Cromwell and McElrath 1994; Sutton 1995).

Living in an area where drug dealers and users are seen as a major problem increases the odds of being offered stolen goods by a factor of 1.6. This is likely to be a reflection of the interrelated nature of stolen goods and illicit drugs markets. In-depth interviews with heroin users revealed that many were particularly active in stealing and selling stolen goods - sometimes hawking them door-to-door around their neighbourhood.

As with buying stolen goods (Chapter 3), a lifestyle based crime-risk score was generated from a number of responses to questions concerning drug use, going out behaviour and heavy drinking. The odds of respondents with a high risk score being offered stolen goods were nearly one and a half times greater than those with a medium or low risk score. The explanation for why people with a higher risk score are more likely to be offered stolen goods is the same as for buying stolen goods: going out to certain pubs and clubs leads to a greater frequency of contact with people involved in crime, which increases contact with people selling stolen goods (Felson 1994).

The odds of being offered stolen goods for those who had carried outside on their person more than £200 of cash in the past month were nearly twice those who carried lesser amounts. However, the influence of this factor is difficult to explain on the basis of survey data alone. It seems likely that it is associated with such influences as: potential sellers having knowledge of the respondent's ability to pay; the respondent being part of a particular type of friendship group where carrying a large 'wad' of money is seen as important; and sellers knowing or believing that customers may be found in such groups.

The odds of those who said they were not managing on their income[49] being offered stolen goods were also significantly higher than for the better off. There are various possible reasons for this including local neighbourhood effects. People living in areas characterised by a high level of unemployment or high crime rates are more likely to experience financial hardship and to be identified by thieves, and others who sell stolen goods, as likely customers for cheaper items such as baby clothes, food, and cigarettes.

---

48   The in-depth interviews with burglars suggested that this is often the case.
49   Just getting by, unable to save or spend on leisure or getting into difficulties (as opposed to managing quite well and able to save or spend on leisure).

Table 5.3 Offered Stolen Goods: final model

Variable	s.s	*odds ratio*
Believe many neighboursown stolen goods	****	2.5
Drugs problem in neighbourhood	****	1.6
Not managing very well on income	**	1.3
ACORN GROUP †		
Rising/Striving	***	1.8
Expanding/Settling/Aspiring	*	1.5
Carried more than £200 of cash in the past month	****	1.7
Easy to recognise a stranger in the neighbourhood	**	1.3
High Risk Score	***	1.4
AGE ‡		
16 - 24	****	6.0
25 - 35	****	2.1
Being Male	****	2.0
Personally know someone who was burgled in past year	****	1.8

s.s *p<0.05 **p<0.01 ***p<0.001 ****P<0.0001
Unweighted data. Source:1994 BCS. Follow-up A sample
† Estimate of the increased odds of being offered stolen goods are compared with Acorn group: *Thriving*
‡ Estimate of the increased odds of being offered stolen goods are compared with Age group 36-60
A fuller version of this table is given in Appendix 1 (Table A1.7).

Due to the wide range of ways in which offers of stolen goods can take place and different interpretations of what it means to be offered stolen goods, the relationship between offers received and actually buying stolen goods is only suggestive of the role played by opportunity in stolen goods markets. A less problematic approach is to use the offered and bought data to look at those who were offered stolen goods, but did not buy any.

Offers declined: further analysis

As was seen from Table 5.2, not all those who said they had been offered stolen goods in the previous 12 months took up the offer. Indeed, over half (56 percent) said that they had never bought any stolen goods over the past five years, let alone 12 months. It appears, from the figures in Table 5.4, that those who said they received more offers of stolen goods also bought most frequently. Seven out of 10 people who said they **often** received offers of stolen goods bought stolen goods. Conversely, more than two thirds of those who said they had been offered stolen goods only once declined.[50]

---

50   The *declined* category cannot take account of those who resisted buying stolen goods more than 12 months ago - some of whom may not have bought stolen goods in the past five years or received any offers to buy in the past year.

Likely customers for stolen goods are probably targeted more frequently and, by receiving more offers, the item they want is more likely to come up. In some cases, those receiving only one offer may have the propensity to buy but just not want the particular item offered. Some people may lose any resolve to decline offers of stolen goods through exposure to many opportunities. Others might simply live in areas where stolen goods markets have been a way of life for generations (Parker et al 1988; Hobbs 1989) and being offered stolen goods is a commonplace or even daily occurrence.

Table 5.4 *Relationship between number of offers and self-reported buying behaviour*

| | Offered stolen goods (past year) | | | | | | | |
| | once | | a few times | | often | | Total | |
	n	%	n	%	n	%	n	%
Bought stolen goods	96	**32**	232	**46**	82	**71**	410	44
Declined	235	**68**	286	**54**	45	**29**	566	56
TOTAL	332	100	518	100	127	100	976	100

Weighted data (unweighted n=976). Excluding don't know and refused answers of which there were 15.

Of those who received at least one offer over the past year, 44 percent bought stolen goods. Not surprisingly, those who said they never received any offers in the past 12 months were significantly less likely to report buying stolen goods in the past five years.[51] It seems, therefore, that there is a considerable degree of *opportunity* influencing buying behaviour (Mayhew et al 1976). For some, this will be happening independently of any previous purchasing behaviour, or buyers seeking out stolen goods. Of course, whether or not individuals are carrying sufficient cash is also likely to be important.

The issue of neighbours buying stolen goods was discussed earlier in Chapter 2. However, the perceived level of ownership of stolen goods in the area where respondents live also appears to be closely connected to the number of offers a person receives and whether or not they buy what is offered.

---

51 This does not take account of earlier offers (more than a year ago) that might have been received by the 595 respondents who said they had not received any offers in the past year and yet bought stolen goods at some time in the past five years.

Table 5.5 *Relationship between perception of proportions of neighbours with stolen goods and being offered stolen goods*

	a lot	a few	not many	none	refused	d.know
	%	%	%	%	%	%
Received offer of stolen goods						
yes	**33**	**21**	**10**	4	9	8
no	67	79	90	96	91	92
Decliners	47	45	64	64	100	67
Unweighted n	408	1588	4217	2210	13	317

Weighted data. Source:1994 BCS.

Table 5.5 shows that those people who believe that their neighbours own stolen goods are also more likely to be offered stolen goods. A similar pattern was found among those who said they had bought stolen goods (Table 2.6). Unfortunately, it is not possible to judge the extent to which belief about neighbours' ownership of stolen goods is influenced by the number of offers a respondent receives. However, the *decliners* category is more helpful: a much higher percentage of those who thought that either 'none' or at least 'not many' of their neighbours had stolen goods were decliners. This reinforces findings discussed earlier about the importance of local area effects on buying behaviour. It seems that people living in areas where fewer neighbours own stolen goods are less likely to be offered stolen goods and, if and when they are offered stolen goods, they are less likely to buy.

Analysis of ACORN areas reveals further differences in terms of being offered stolen goods and declining to buy. The highest proportion of decliners came from the Rising areas (affluent urbanites, town and city areas, prosperous professionals in metropolitan areas and better-off executives in inner city areas). As Table 5.6 shows, almost seven out of 10 respondents in Rising areas declined to buy stolen goods in the past year. By way of contrast, five out of 10 in Striving areas declined to buy.

Table 5.6 *Acorn categories by level of involvement with stolen goods[52]*

		Thriving	Expanding	Rising	Settling	Aspiring	Striving
Offered	%	7	9	12	11	13	17
	N	(90)	(94)	(84)	(230)	(146)	(333)
Declined	%	57	59	69	54	57	51
	N	(53)	(60)	(59)	(127)	(84)	(184)

Weighted percentages. Unweighted N. The % of decliners is based on those who were offered stolen goods.

---

52   The percentages in this table have been rounded upwards. Although the *offered* and *bought* figures are almost identical - this is coincidental as not all those who were offered bought, as can be seen by the figures for *decliners*.

The BCS data on reported buying stolen goods do not distinguish between buying in the local area or further afield. Opportunities to buy stolen goods also exist away from where people live, and if it were otherwise the ACORN effect shown might possibly have been greater.[53] Some people buy stolen goods as a result of chance encounters with thieves and other handlers away from their immediate neighbourhood. A historical study of the black economy in Britain provides an interesting example of how this happened to businessmen buying stolen social security stamps in London in 1934 (Smithies 1984):

> ...*many purchasers of stolen stamps were traced when the address book of a dealer was found. According to the police such 'dealers' persuaded gangs of youths to break into offices to steal the cards. The existence of a 'ready market' was the motive but the businessmen who bought the stamps had invariably had accidental encounters with the 'agents' or 'dealers' who sold them. They met in billiard halls, pubs, at boxing matches, coffee stalls, in tube trains and railway stations and on one occasion in a public lavatory.*

Limitations of the findings so far

Although analysis was undertaken to examine the relationship between opportunity (offers) to buy stolen goods and offending (buying the stolen goods), the results must be treated with a degree of caution. There are two main reasons for this: firstly, respondents were only asked about offers of stolen goods in the past year but about buying stolen goods over a five-year period. Therefore, it is not possible to determine accurately what proportion of those buying stolen goods were also offered stolen goods, because they may have received an offer more than a year ago. Secondly, the relatively large percentage of buyers saying they had been offered stolen goods might, in part, result from some respondents telescoping experiences of being offered stolen goods from previous years (more than a year ago) into the survey. For others, forgetfulness rather than telescoping might have influenced the findings. In such cases, any association between the number of offers a respondent says they have received and the number of times they have bought stolen goods would be exaggerated. Equally, it is possible that at least some of those who said they had never received an offer, and had never bought stolen goods, had actually bought items two to five years ago but had forgotten about them. Therefore, the incidence of buying stolen goods is likely to be an underestimate compared with the incidence of being offered

---

53   In some cases, the least well off cannot afford to buy stolen goods even if they want them. This also means that the ACORN effect is not as powerful as might otherwise be expected.

stolen goods. This may be partly offset, however, by the fact that incidents of buying stolen goods are more likely to be remembered than unaccepted offers.

Demand and supply

Research in Canada (Tremblay et al 1994) found that changes in rates of unrecovered stolen vehicles were influenced by a number of factors which increased the price of cars and car parts. In effect, people were more likely to buy stolen cars for their own use, and garages were more likely to use stolen car parts in repairs, when market regulations made legitimate cars and parts significantly more expensive.

It seems that this same principle probably applies to all electrical goods. They fetch high prices when the retail price is high, but when prices fall the demand also falls as stolen goods markets become saturated with equipment. Once high street prices become affordable for those with low incomes, legitimate electrical goods become more desirable than stolen ones. One of the interviewees dealt as a Residential fence for stolen VCRs during the period when the demand for them was at its peak. At this time he sold VCRs on commission for inexperienced burglars. The peak period was said to have been four to five years after they first appeared on the market:

> *They was being taken from what I call richer houses to, basically, council houses. It was really greed, greed, greed. Especially when there weren't many of 'em out. And then, basically, the shops started selling cheap. Discounts, and HP and everything. Even the poor have them now, on weekly payments.*

More recently, the same thing happened to mobile phones as one of the YOI sample explained:

> *I used to be well into mobile phones when they first came out. I used to get a hundred pounds, hundred and fifty pounds a mobile phone. But now you can pick 'em up in the shops for like ten or fifteen quid. So they're not worth fuck-all now. It's all gone, completely gone.*

When this happens to particular types of goods they become less attractive to thieves because they are harder to sell and fetch less money. Conversely, if demand increases for particular products, they become more attractive to thieves.

Stolen VCRs can still be sold, usually for between £30 and £50. Compared to the 1980s, when they fetched around £100, the current price-to-weight ratio means that it is now hardly 'worth the risk' of stealing, transporting and selling them unless they are top of the range models. When asked whether they had experienced difficulty selling particular types of stolen goods, several burglars referred to this decline in the market for VCRs:

> *I mean you used to be able to get seventy or eighty pound for a video seven years ago - and now you would be lucky to get fifteen or twenty for it, because you can buy a video for seventy to eighty pound brand new. You've got to look at the end of the scale there. They [potential buyers] say: "Well look I can get a video from a shop brand new no problems and I'm not going to get no trouble about it."*

The two factors which seem particularly to influence demand for stolen electrical goods are the price of legitimate goods and the newness of the technology. When VCRs first appeared on the market, any that were being sold second-hand would have been known to be 'virtually new', and consumers would be very unlikely to have a model at home. When 'revolutionary' new products such as colour television sets, VCRs and mobile phones first arrived in the high street shops at expensive prices they quickly became popular targets for burglars. Their presence **might** well have increased the overall incidence of burglary and other thefts by making these crimes particularly attractive propositions (see Sutton 1995).

Elasticity of demand

Supply and demand is another area which has an important bearing on the way stolen goods markets operate. Inelastic demand means that a relatively high increase in price will not substantially lower sales volume (see Reuter 1985; Edmunds et al 1996). This is what can be called a 'sellers' market'. Elastic demand, on the other hand, has the opposite effect and creates a buyers' market.

The concept of elasticity of demand may be useful in terms of predicting the type of goods thieves will prioritise. From a crime prevention perspective, being able to predict which goods will be characterised by inelastic demand[54] could have considerable pay-offs if they were singled out for special anti-theft attention. Such goods could be made less stealable at the point of manufacture, retail or installation. It is worth mentioning at this point that Bennett and Wright (1984) found that one of the main concerns of burglars was to spend as little time as possible in the building. So

---

54   Predicting which goods are likely to be targeted by thieves is a subject addressed more broadly by Ekblom (1997).

manufacturers of goods which are likely to be sold in markets where demand is inelastic could help to reduce theft by designing products to make them harder to find and steal. For example, facilitating remote siting in unexpected or hidden areas.

Stolen goods, in general, are likely to be quite elastic in that a substantial increase in price will deter buyers who have to break the law, pay in cash, and risk that the goods might be faulty. However, markets for stolen jewellery are influenced by world market prices and are much less sensitive to local demand and supply.

Prices

Stolen goods are not always sold for less than the retail price (Reuter 1990). A Commercial fence can sell stolen jewellery in his jeweller's shop for the same price as legitimate jewellery (Walsh 1977). Dealers in second-hand goods and corner shop owners can do the same (Steffensmeier 1986). However, goods sold through Residential fences, Network sales and Hawking are invariably sold considerably below the normal retail price. The thief who sells to a fence usually gets less money than if he/she sells directly to the consumer.

The interviewees who were engaged in stealing and redistributing stolen goods were all very knowledgeable of the prices of expensive electrical goods. In some cases, respondents walked around big department stores to establish retail prices. Two of the interviewees said that their Residential fence used a catalogue to work out prices. Another used a catalogue herself to ensure she was receiving a 'fair' price:

> *Basically the best thing I used to go by was the Argos catalogue. Have one of them handy whatever you are going to steal. A lot of people are going to buy from Argos anyway. I used to go through, find the price and basically used to work at half the price, then it went to a third and from a third to negotiable...*

Selling stolen goods: the 'two and three way split'

For many years there has been a general rule of thumb that the thief will be paid one third of the retail price of either new or 'nearly new' second-hand stolen goods (Quennell 1962). Steffensmeier (1986), who found that this practice had gone on even before the 19th century, also points out that experienced thieves are more likely to ask for half the wholesale price, or base their asking price on the fence's selling prices. Walsh (1977) found that fast-moving consumer goods attracted more stable prices, with thieves being paid 30 to 40 percent of the retail price for stolen cigarettes.

From police interviews with 115 fences in the USA, Walsh (1977) found that although drug misusers and inexperienced thieves might get paid less, generally thieves got paid 30 to 50 percent of wholesale prices. The price of goods would rise, to beat competition from other fences, when the market was buoyant and there were a number of competitors for what was being sold.

Some types of goods, for which a Residential fence or consumer might pay one third of the retail price, would not be purchased for the same price by a Commercial fence with access to the legitimate wholesale market place; it depends on the normal wholesale-to-retail mark-up of goods (see Steffensmeier 1986). Jewellery, for instance, has a high mark-up and the jeweller-fence would be better off buying jewellery wholesale than stolen jewellery - which would cost one third of the retail price.[55] That is why most stolen jewellery is sold by thieves for the scrap metal price. Electrical goods have a much smaller mark-up, and the Commercial fence can still make a good profit by paying a third of the retail price. As one male heroin user explained:

> *The thief charges a third to the fence, and he'll put like an extra five to ten pound on it, whatever. What he knows he can get for it. He'll probably go for half price the value of the goods, 'cos the ticket is usually on the stuff. He'll go for the half price, and half price to somebody [the consumer] is worth it, but the thief usually has to sell it at a third.*

Shoplifters who hawked stolen clothes tended to charge half the retail price. However, when thieves sold clothes to Residential fences living locally, the one third rule was applied. This ensured the consumer would still get that half price 'bargain'.

One interviewee explained how he sometimes sold the clothes through a network of Residential fences:

> *Say we got a good brand name like Armani or something like that, now we go in at a third. Bang a third on it if it's decent and then they'll give it out to a couple of people charging halves. Say they've bought a parcel of Valentino shirts - they're eighty quid a shirt. They're going to go out and do them for forty quid. That's just doing bits of it like in the estates and that. People taking a carrier bag of stuff out with them and going around their friends' houses*

---

55   For a contrary view see Wright and Decker (1984: 170) where an informant told them that a fifteen hundred dollar watch could be sold to a fence for a third or a quarter of this retail value.

or whatever. There's a lot of other people involved in this sort of thing. It's going to end up all around the area.

One female heroin user was an accomplished shoplifter with a number of regular customers. She provided information which matches Walsh's (1977) findings that fast-moving consumer goods were sold to a fence for half the retail price:

The thing is, usually everything is a third. Say for instance, if I got you a jumper for fifty pounds, I would do it for a third. But with meat you can get half the price. It doesn't matter what meat it is they will buy it. So you go for the most expensive pieces of joints. Go in, fill carrier bags, and go back four or five times.

This half price rule for fast-moving consumer goods appeared to be almost 'cast in stone'. A male heroin user had been dealing in drugs and would exchange drugs to the equivalent value of half the retail price for meat and large bottles of spirits:

"With booze and meat it's half, with anything else it's a third."

For expensive car stereos, the thieves usually got paid between a third and a half of the retail value. Although half the retail value was seen as fairer by some of the interviewees, most, but not all, were happy to accept a third. Another male heroin user exclaimed:

I don't like this third business, that's why me and thieving never got on really. I'm putting my flipping liberty up here. I want a bit more.

Cars and motor bikes were either sold to third parties or scrapped for considerably less than second-hand market value. Stolen cars, regardless of age or make, were generally scrapped at between £30 and £200. There were three respondents in the sample who, for a while, specialised in stealing and scrapping motor vehicles. Each said they had developed a close working relationship with their dealer to avoid detection. Cars that were only five years old with a second-hand market value of around £5,000 were being sold to scrap yards for £250:

If you're talking today you can get like up to a J reg in certain scrap yards - in others you're talking like a C. They just rip 'em apart and crush 'em. I mean I have had a few people that ringed[56] 'em like but they're few and far between. I mean I know you hear a lot about it but you don't get a lot of it. Most of 'em just get ripped

---

56   Used a stolen car and a legitimate, damaged, car to create one 'cloned' car for sale to an often unsuspecting purchaser.

apart. More for spare parts. Even then the expensive ones are getting scrapped as well, they just rip 'em to pieces and crush the body. You know, they're making a fortune on the bits.

Overall then, second-hand items were usually sold by the thief for a third of the retail value. If the thief sells to a Residential fence, the fence sells to a consumer for half the retail value. Goods sold to second-hand shops are usually sold-on to the public for two-thirds of the retail value - depending upon their condition. Gold jewellery sold to jewellery shops is usually sold at the going rate for scrap gold.

It is interesting to note that cheque books and credit cards are exempt from the characteristic 'two and three way split'. The price paid for cheque books and credit cards was much wider in range, but they changed hands for relatively little money. The price range for each cheque, with a guarantee card, was between £3 and £11. They were usually sold in books, not singly. These prices are virtually identical to those found by Levi et al (1991).[57] One of the interviewees said that when cheques were sold at the lower range, the card might also be worth an additional £20. The going price for a credit card was around £25. Buyers have to take it on trust that cheque books have been recently stolen and that high street shops have not yet been notified. This probably explains why, despite having so much purchasing power, cheques, cheque cards and credit cards are sold so cheaply.

Quick and satisfactory sales

Most thieves sold in a variety of different ways. Selling methods were dependent upon: level of experience; patience; drug use; current relationships with others - thieves or fences; and the type of goods. Less experienced and less prolific thieves used one buyer only and accepted whatever price they were offered for goods. The least experienced often had trouble finding a buyer. Two interviewees from the YLS sample said that at times they had to dump stolen VCRs and computers on waste ground and in rivers because they could not find a buyer (see also Maguire 1982: 71). Car and motorcycle thieves invariably dealt with one scrap yard at a time. Those who had been arrested and sentenced for doing this said that they had then changed their offending to burglary and stealing components from cars as they felt that scrap yards were being too closely watched.[58] More experienced thieves had access to a broader range of outlets so that when a fence was arrested, or started reducing prices or limiting what they would buy (either demanding bulk purchases or rejecting certain items), they did not have to alter their rate of offending accordingly.

---

57   Between £3 and £10 per cheque.
58   These components, such as car tyres or even engines, were then sold directly to consumers.

Using a reliable fence ensured that thieves could sell stolen goods quickly and at prices they usually felt were fair. However, they sometimes sold at prices which they felt were too low (see also Wright and Decker 1994), either because they had nowhere else to take them or because they did not want to go back out on to the 'streets' and risk being arrested in possession.

Several factors affect the need for a quick sale. The least experienced and less active thieves tended to be in less of a hurry. Those who had only committed one or two burglaries, and those recounting their first burglaries, described holding on to stolen goods for a number of weeks while seeking out a buyer. Not surprisingly, those who regularly used heroin and cocaine were keen to sell stolen goods as quickly as possible and were also least interested in securing better prices. As a group, these drug users were more likely to have been arrested for possessing stolen goods, probably because they were such prolific thieves and also because at times they were willing to run higher risks.

To protect themselves from being caught in possession, thieves often hid stolen goods for a few hours until they could be collected and transported to a buyer (see also Kock et al 1996). Some offenders resorted to burying stolen goods and using lock-up garages. Higher prices may be obtained for stolen goods where the thief is prepared to store them and sell under favourable conditions. Walsh (1977) found that stolen clothing was most likely to be stored in a spare room at home but (presumably) some are wary of doing this:

> I wouldn't have nothing in my house. I used to have it all in someone else's house and I'd give them the key and they used to go out. And what they could sell they take with 'em and write it down in a book and I know what's gone...do it like that.

Where thefts had been committed specifically to buy drugs, thieves were generally content to exchange stolen goods either directly for drugs, or for a mixture of cash and drugs. Those who exchanged goods for drugs felt that they got more drugs by doing this than by selling goods for cash and using the cash to spend on drugs:

> If I could get drugs instead of cash I would take the drugs. Because at the end of the day that's what I wanted and because if anybody is selling me drugs it usually means that they've got a large amount of drugs. So it usually means that they will give you more drugs for the stuff.

Other respondents were of the opinion that exchanging goods for drugs was a 'mugs' game' and that only the desperate resorted to this measure.

However, accounts provided by many interviewees suggest that swapping goods for drugs and getting less drugs than the cash equivalent for the goods merely reflected the value attached to getting hold of drugs at the time you want them. Most of those who swapped stolen goods for drugs did not feel bad about being 'ripped off'. Drug dealers were able to exploit thieves whose desire for drugs often outweighed their desire for money:

> *I have sold like a top range video for forty pounds worth of crack. And that was to a drug dealer. Whereas, if I'd waited 'till the morning I'd have got a hundred pound on that. I just wanted to smoke some crack and I can't be bothered. You definitely get a worse deal if you swap goods for drugs.*

One interviewee, who had dealt speed and cocaine from his flat, explained the drug dealer's perspective on accepting stolen goods for drugs:

> *I used to sell to small time dealers who used to have say an ounce a week. They couldn't pay me until they sold it, see. I'd lay it on them and they'd bring it to me [the money] on Friday. A number of times they'd come around with videos and cars when they owed me money. I wasn't happy about it, but you would have to get me three videos for eighty quid [eighty pounds worth of drugs].*

The role of entrepreneurs

Many of the more prolific offenders had increased their offending considerably in the period leading up to their latest conviction. These 'crime sprees' came after they had already been arrested more than once. By this stage they had usually developed specific criminal techniques, were specialising in particular types of burglary and had established relationships with a fence. One adult burglar described his relationship with a newly found Residential fence after he had just received a suspended prison sentence and how his offending increased as a result:

> *In the end I was just at it all the time. He [the Residential fence] was introducing me to a lot of people. 'Though they lived in a poor area of council houses a lot of the people were sometimes thieves themselves. Some people just wanted to sell on again and he was selling to a buyer who was selling to another buyer.*

Careers

Some interviewees failed to sell items they had stolen in their first burglaries (see also Maguire 1982) and never committed more than two or three before giving it up. However, where a burglar's early burglaries resulted in the successful conversion of stolen property into cash, this invariably led to further burglaries. Criminal 'career' choices of this kind could be explained simply in terms of rewards-based behaviour, but are probably more complex. The existence of established markets and provision of guidance from experienced offenders are likely to be almost essential local conditions for them to make successful sales. The effect of early success or failure to convert stolen property into cash is an important area. Reducing markets for stolen goods might curtail many criminal careers before they 'take off'.

Careers of those interviewed tended to follow similar pathways. Involvement in serious acquisitive crime (e.g. burglary, car theft etc) tended to develop during the mid teens. In each case where offenders found a 'fair' and efficient fence their new sources of income helped only to entrench their offending behaviour, especially if they were using drugs. Excessive use of drugs and alcohol was fuelled by acquisitive offending which was becoming increasingly reckless, including doing night-time burglaries ('creepers') when householders were asleep, shop robberies and ram-raiding. One adult burglar's criminal career was prematurely terminated by open heart surgery at the age of 26. He said doctors believed that his heart condition might have been caused by his lifestyle and drug use. Another young burglar had been leading a chaotic lifestyle which terminated when he crashed a stolen car.

Transporting stolen goods

Some respondents used their own cars to get to a burglary and to transport stolen goods (see also Munro, 1972: 32, 35). Others used public transport to go into city centres in search of mountain bikes and would ride the bikes home. One used stolen cars to travel to steal other cars, to commit ram-raids, or to burgle shops and offices. Others walked, or rode on bikes, to commit burglaries and steal car stereos. Black plastic bin bags, sheets and pillow cases found in victims' houses were universally employed by burglars to wrap and carry stolen goods during transportation (see also Wright and Decker (1994).

The use of taxis by thieves was a recurring theme throughout the interviews (see also Kock et al 1996: 5) and six respondents said that they regularly used taxis to take them to burglary sites and to transport stolen goods. Indeed, mini cab[59] drivers were targeted during Operation Bumblebee:

The wide use of mini cabs by burglars is a feature which has caused concern to Operation Bumblebee. On occasions the mini

---

59   Private hire taxis - not licensed (black cabs) 'Hackney' carriages.

cabs have waited outside an address while it is being burgled by their fare. In a large number of cases there is compelling evidence to suggest the driver knows this is happening. (unpublished Metropolitan Police report).

Interviewees who said they used taxis to take them to and from burglaries, or to transport stolen goods, invariably described them as private hire/mini cabs. One burglar explained how he would commit a burglary and then telephone a mini-cab firm from the burgled house to come and pick him up. In this case, the driver never knew that he was transporting a burglar or stolen goods (see also Benney 1936: 311). Some of the respondents who regularly used taxis said they had formed partnerships with the driver - hiring them for the day, paying them a flat rate of £50, or cutting them in on a percentage of the haul:

My mate works as a cab driver and I'll take him and we go halves on whatever we make. Like he's the driver. I prefer to do that really because, like, his risk is if he gets stopped he's got to say the stuff's his. That's how he makes his money. Ten times out of ten he won't get stopped. But 'cause, like, he don't look dodgy enough 'cause he's got an aerial in the back of his car; when police see the aerial they think he's a cabby and don't pull him over. Cabs are safer. Whereas when they see me, I look young and that. I always get stopped. Yeh it's better when I take my mate out in the cab and that.

If I pick the house, I say pull up next to the house. I'll pick a house and I'll go back to his car and I'll say 'yeh there's a telly, video, stack system', and he'll like back the car up and do it double parked or whatever and I'll run in and bring out the goods and put them in his boot and get in the car and we're off.

None of the interviewees mentioned transporting goods over long distances. Goods were sold as quickly as possible to avoid being caught in possession. However, some Residential fences might sell goods over longer distances (see Kock et al 1996).

Summary and Conclusions

Stolen goods markets share many characteristics of legitimate markets. Thieves need to employ simple marketing strategies - targeting particular people and places - to offer stolen goods to those who are most likely to buy. Demand and supply are key factors determining price and, ultimately, the type of goods stolen. There are general rules which determine the percentage of retail prices paid to thieves and profit margins for fences.

Motivation, experience and expertise enabled thieves and fences to maximise income within these rules. Transportation and storage issues are also important in terms of avoiding detection and maximising the price for which goods are sold.

There is some evidence to support suggestions that 'private hire' taxis are used extensively by thieves to transport stolen goods.

There is also some evidence to suggest that buying stolen goods is linked to 'opportunity' through offers received from thieves and Residential fences. Thieves more often offer stolen goods to younger people. They make more offers to males than females and once offered, younger males are less likely to decline than younger females. Those responsible for developing and implementing crime prevention initiatives should take account of this. Chapter 9 outlines how particular situational crime prevention approaches might work to reduce each of the main stolen goods markets.

Identifying which new types of consumer goods will be characterised by inelastic demand might have considerable pay-offs if the public are made aware of their 'stealability' and are encouraged to make such items less attractive. This could be done by using property marking techniques to disfigure desirable goods (see Chapter 9). However, agreement would need to reached with manufacturers that if done in an approved manner warranties would remain valid.

Ambitious fences who sell stolen goods as fast as they can be stolen appear to have a considerable influence on the incidence of offending. Concentrating resources on such 'successful' distributors is likely to reduce overall levels of theft. It may also reduce the number of offenders entering criminal careers since making it even harder to identify a buyer may effectively nip a potential burglar's career in the bud. Similarly, identifying and concentrating resources on 'fair' and reliable fences is likely to make theft less rewarding and thereby reduce both the number of new thieves embarking on criminal careers and the number of offences committed by previously well motivated thieves.

6 DISTINGUISHING CHARACTERISTICS OF STOLEN GOODS MARKETS

While sharing many of the characteristics of legitimate markets, stolen goods markets are fundamentally different because they are illegal. This illegality means that distributors are constrained in many ways and need to adopt clandestine solutions to particular operational problems, such as storing and transporting goods.

This chapter examines some of the distinguishing characteristics of stolen goods markets. The aim here is to identify ways to reduce the number of acquisitive offenders and offences. Understanding more about the behaviour and concerns of distributors and consumers will facilitate and improve the identification of those involved in stolen goods markets and hopefully inform future initiatives aimed at reducing the incidence of handling stolen goods and theft.

Stolen goods markets tend to be small

It would be wrong to think in terms of a single market for stolen goods (see Walsh 1977, Maguire 1982, Reuter 1985). A thief selling to a fence constitutes one market; a thief selling directly to final consumers represents another market; and a fence selling to consumers is another market again. These markets for stolen goods are small and fragmented. The reasons for the small size of illegal markets is explained by Reuter (1985). Focusing on particular types of illegal markets in the United States, he draws useful conclusions about the structure and organisation of drugs markets, 'numbers rackets', 'bootlegging' and gambling operations, explaining why they cannot expand like their legal counterparts:

> *The most immediate consequence of product illegality, stemming from the costs of asset seizure and arrest, is the need to control the*

*flow of information about participation in the illegal activity. That
is, each participant must structure his or her activities, particularly
those involving other participants, so as to assure that the risk of
the police learning of his or her participation is kept low.*

Those involved in selling legitimate goods are able to expand their enterprise
by recruiting employees. However, this is more difficult in illicit markets. For
example, employees may have knowledge of the entrepreneur's criminal
activities and might provide information that can lead to his or her arrest
(Reuter 1985).

Stolen property markets are similar to heroin markets in that they involve
transactions conducted at 'arm's length'. The markets operate at different
levels rather than as a large integrated organisation of stealing, warehousing,
wholesaling and retailing (Reuter 1985, 1990). Although Reuter never
looked at stolen property markets, they share many of the same
characteristics of the various illegal markets he studied.

Morality and criminal motivation

Perceptions of the morality of stealing goods might also influence supply and
demand. The fact that otherwise seemingly law-abiding individuals buy
stolen goods may serve to legitimise theft in the sense that it may neutralise
feelings of guilt associated with stealing (see Sykes and Matza 1957). This
readiness to buy among the public also appears to serve as an underlying
motivation for thieves to take advantage of opportunities that present
themselves (Parker 1974, Mayhew et al 1976) - not so much going out on
theft forays but sometimes stealing just because the chance to make money
turns up.

In terms of the morality of buying, knowing that so many people buy stolen
goods may also serve to justify such acts or to reduce feelings of guilt:
'everyone else is buying so why not me' or 'if I don't buy it someone else
will' (Cromwell et al 1991).

One interviewee, for example, believed that everyone in his neighbourhood
was buying stolen goods and was prepared to buy whenever the right
opportunity presented itself:

*You see the whole place is the same, the whole village is the same.
Everyone buys stuff, even the straight people who have never done
anything wrong, never been in trouble in their life. It's like me next
door neighbours: dead normal couple, never been in trouble,
nothing like me or anything - they buy stuff. It's down to money*

every single time. If something's cheap, they're selling at half price -
you're saving yourself money.

Violence and vigilantism

The opportunities available to save and make money through buying and
selling stolen goods are not without danger. Markets for stolen goods will, at
times, be characterised by violence. As Reuter (1985) points out:

> *...participants in illegal markets lack recourse to state facilities for*
> *dispute settlement. Violence or threats may provide the only*
> *method of resolving disputes in at least some situations.*

One adult burglar related how such a confrontation had led to imprisonment
for himself and his friend. Since moving to a new address, they had both
committed six burglaries within two weeks, and were selling stolen goods
through network sales:

> *Another geezer that was sharing this house. He was a boxer. Quite*
> *a big bloke. And he come down one day. He bought a stereo off*
> *[X][60] and it didn't work. He started hitting him about - and [X]*
> *weren't small, he was about 13 stone - and he gave him one*
> *almighty whack in our room. For some reason he took the Samurai*
> *sword off the wall and started hitting him [the boxer].*

> *We had to call an ambulance. It went to court and my friend got*
> *off with it as self defence. When the police came back the next day*
> *they checked the goods in the house (stereo, portable tv, jewellery*
> *etc). I didn't think about having stolen goods in the house and that.*
> *They took all the numbers and that and they came back that night*
> *as I was walking into the house with some shopping with my*
> *girlfriend. They said: "You're under arrest for burglary". In fact,*
> *they only charged us with three burglaries and we pleaded guilty to*
> *'em. [X] got 15 months and at the same time I got 18 months*
> *[prison sentences]."*

Other instances of violence were mentioned by a male respondent who had
himself committed domestic burglaries and had served six month's
imprisonment for burglary. He described how heroin users, who were
blamed for burglaries locally, would be punished by local 'toughs':

> *If there's ever a burglary you find out who it was 'cause you know*

---

60   The respondent's friend and eventual co-defendant.

who they are. They're mostly smack heads and you get the stuff back and give them a good hiding.

A female heroin user had herself been confronted by locals on enough occasions to know that drug users were the focus of immediate suspicion when burglaries were committed in the neighbourhood:

I wouldn't buy somethin' that I know somebody's robbed out of a house - 'specially local. Because y'know not only would the police come or whatever, but you could have gangs of fellas knocking on your door - y'know what I mean.

Say like you tend to, like, know who the local burglars are. So say, like, someone's house got robbed or whatever and say it's so-and-so's house, or they're related to so-and-so, then they're likely to grab hold of one of them and find out who they sold it to.

You'll have like a type of burglar who'll rob anyone and anything. That sort of person, I wouldn't trust - they'd get me done [arrested]. I wouldn't want to get involved because as I say, then you get a name. Then you never know, you could be in bed one day and someone could burst in.

Even where legitimate channels for redress exist, some locals in high crime neighbourhoods by-passed these systems, preferring instead to seize back stolen goods themselves and to inflict physical punishment on offenders. Given the level of ownership identified by the BCS, in many cases this probably happens where the very goods that are stolen had actually been purchased from thieves, and the latest 'victim' is afraid that the police might discover this and so is unlikely to report the theft. This factor might also partially explain the low take-up of property marking schemes in certain areas (Laycock 1985).

Morality of self-interest

Within the moral framework described above, burglary of factories and shops is acceptable, and shoplifting is acceptable - but burglary on the estate is 'wrong'. Several respondents expressed the importance of not 'doing it' on your own doorstep (see also Parker 1974; Stone 1975). However, there are exceptions, and one of the heroin users explained how sometimes it was difficult to abide by this ethic:

Like I said shitting on your own doorstep - when I was actually at the start [of burglary career] I was already on the drugs when doing it [burglary]. And then it became the need ...that I needed the drugs. So I was out robbing on a withdrawal. I tended to find that I used to rob the next door neighbours to where I was living[61] because I didn't have the energy. The first score of the day to get up and travel. I just wanted to score, but after I'd done the first one I probably would travel.

Parker (1974: 84) explains how 'selective local citizenship' leads to the condemnation of local burglars. Such condemnation is more likely to occur in close knit communities (Parker 1974: 85) where: 'Respect is related to some form of meaningful commitment, at the very least the expediency of having too much to lose of one's own.' A similar 'morality of self-interest', among drug dealers, was outlined by one of the burglars interviewed from the YOI sample who said that he had to reduce his offending on his own estate because the dealers were worried about the police presence it was attracting. These local drug dealers told him that they would break the legs of the person doing it if ever they found out who it was.

While this protective commitment exists between established residents, it does not so often extend to newcomers who may be fair game for burglary (see also Foster and Hope 1993). As one interviewee explained:

I suppose it's just because they're new, because nobody knows who they are. Plus like when you rob someone on here you never know who you're robbing. Like if some smack head from a different area comes on here right, there's a lot of like heavy [tough] people on here and you could be like nicking off a mate of a heavy person. You don't take the risk of doing it. But when someone new comes on, they're from a different area. It's a target where they don't know anyone and they're going to be alright [no retaliation]. 'Cause most people on here don't like burglars, even though they do buy stuff. They don't like burglars, it's, a bit daft really. Even though you don't agree with people burgling houses and yet you're willing to buy the stuff out of it. It all comes down to the money doesn't it. It's just people... how to make money, that's why you've got people buying stolen goods and that.

Summary and Conclusions

Stolen goods markets are unable to expand very far as they need to remain hidden from the attentions of law-abiding members of the public and particularly the police. Thus, they are most likely to be small, local and transitory. They may at times be characterised by episodes of apparently

---

61   See also Wright and Decker (1994).

unexplained violence or intimidation. Therefore, from a policing perspective, it might sometimes be worthwhile looking behind the scenes of particular reported violent episodes between neighbours and acquaintances to determine whether disagreements over stolen goods transactions are to blame. Witnesses (even victims) of such episodes might also be more actively encouraged to report them to the police.

In housing areas where newcomers tend to be consistently victimised, established residents should be encouraged to extend the same lack of tolerance to this behaviour as they would if it were happening to the neighbours they know. One approach might be to develop a scheme whereby newcomers are taken around an estate and introduced to popular and respected members of the community.

7 WHAT HAPPENS TO STOLEN GOODS

To see the precise way that distributors and consumers reap benefits from using products stolen from others, it is necessary to look in more detail at what happens to stolen goods. This chapter provides further insight into what motivates offenders to steal and buy stolen goods. Using three diverse examples - car stereos, cheques and credit cards, and jewellery - it looks at what typically happens to such goods and where they end up. Most types of stolen goods are usually sold in ways similar to at least one of these examples.

Car stereos

Thefts of car stereo systems account for a substantial proportion of all crimes committed. The 1996 British Crime Survey (Mirrlees-Black et al 1996) found that thefts from cars accounted for 13 percent of all offences. This figure is almost four times higher than thefts from cars reported to the police. Nearly a third of these thefts were of car stereo equipment. Car stereo theft appears to cause considerable personal hardship, since few people claim for replacement costs from their insurers. Only 63 percent of car crime victims had insurance which covered theft from their cars and only 17 percent of those who have something stolen from their car claim on their policy. Pengelly (1996) explains why so many people do not claim on their insurance when their car stereo systems are stolen:

> *Victims of these thefts are placed in a dilemma over whether to make a claim from their insurers. Very often, insurers will not pay the first hundred or more pounds of the claim and this, coupled with the potential loss of no claims discounts, leaves the victim with little choice but to replace the stolen system with a 'second-hand' one. Of course, some of these second-hand stereos may have been stolen.*

Criminologists have studied car radio thieves to provide some explanation for why they steal and how they sell them (Parker 1974):

> *The Boys' delinquent action was largely determined by the availability of illegitimate opportunities of which they might choose to take advantage. ...several factors encouraged their choice in becoming car radio thieves. The radios were available in large supply, a middlemen service was on hand to exchange stolen property for money and the neighbourhood tended to turn a blind eye to such infractions. What's more, the street corner milieu actually encouraged such action and provided a continuous flow of helpful information.*

Car stereo thefts have increased considerably in recent years, but what happens to them remains something of a mystery. Kock et al (1996) interviewed police officers and civilian police staff and noted:

> *Several officers expressed amazement at the number of car radios that were stolen in their divisions and wondered how such numbers were finding buyers.*

As stereo radio-cassette systems have been fitted as a standard feature in cars for many years now, it is unclear why they should be stolen at all (Pengelly 1996). 'What happens to stolen car stereos?' has become a frequently asked question. The following section attempts to answer it.

Car stereos 'worth' stealing

Car stereo systems become increasingly sophisticated each year. The latest and best in-car entertainment equipment is desirable but at the same time can be prohibitively expensive. The high street prices of such equipment push it beyond the reach of many young people who desire, or believe they 'require', the best and latest equipment as a status symbol. This creates a demand for such equipment at 'affordable' prices.

Almost half of those interviewed had been involved in redistributing stolen car stereos. The stereos they stole and sold had to be top of the range models to have any real value. One of the respondents from the YLS sample said:

> *Sometimes we'd nick radios and they weren't worth that [snaps fingers]. They weren't worth nuffink.*

Valuable stereos had to be sought out. A 20-year-old in the YOI sample described the amount of effort and planning that such theft forays sometimes involved:

> *I used to go out all night on my own and get about 10 stereos. Sometimes I'd be out to five o'clock in the morning, or six o'clock in the morning. Wake up at two when it's dead outside. Come out. Know where your hunting grounds are[62] ...so you know where to go back at night-time. Sometimes I'd go out on a mountain bike, other times on foot. Chances are you ain't gonna get seen.*

Two young males, both of whom lived with their parents, bought car stereo systems for their own use and had also bought many others to sell. One regularly bought and sold stereos, but said he had never stolen any:

> *I don't make me living selling car stereos but when there's a chance to do it you do it. I'd rather keep 'em like, but you can't keep all these stereos can you. I've had a lot of stereos[63] and they were all good... It's me hobby really[64], I just like stereos.*

He began buying stolen stereos for his first car, which had a stereo already installed when he first bought it. Asked why he bought a stolen stereo to replace this existing model he said:

> *...because it were better. The one that were in it were a crap'n.[65] I like stereos, I like systems, I'm always trying to better me car stereo.*

He then left the room and fetched from the kitchen the removable face[66] from the stolen stereo that he currently had in his car:

> *This is one I've got at the moment. That's stolen. It's one of the best you can get. It's Alpine, clip off front. That's £695 to buy. It's style, Alpine. That's a really good make that.*

This expensive stereo had been bought from a friend for £100. His parents knew that he had a stolen stereo in his car. He said that all his mates knew as well. When asked if he was concerned about this he said that his only worry was that his mates might find out how much he actually paid for it because he might want to sell it to them for a profit. He was currently in the process of selling a Sony stereo through a friend who was going to buy it off him for £60 so that he could in turn sell it on for £70. Such small profit margins were

---

62 See Wright and Decker (1994) - Many of their informants found targets in the day-time and returned to steal them later.
63 Approximately 20.
64 Said without a trace of irony.
65 Quite basic and definitely not top of the range.
66 This feature is meant to prevent theft of the system. The face should be removed from the car whenever the owner leaves it unattended.

typical (see Reuter 1990).

The other interviewee explained why he felt he had to replace the stereo that came with his first car two years earlier:

> *It came with a really shit radio fitted in, like a MW LW cassette. It was not powerful enough, the quality isn't there. It hasn't got the functions because it didn't have a rewind button - it only had fast-forward.*

He also had quite a few stolen stereos in his house at one time:

> *...It was quite funny because I had a bag of car stereos hidden in my bedroom. I knew I could get rid of them if I really wanted to. Some of them were good quality and some were not as good as I thought they would be looking through the glass. I sold them all through friends.*

Due to their size, car stereos are easy to conceal and store in this way. However, they do not appear to stay in one place for a particularly long time. For almost half of those interviewed - stealing, selling, collecting and trading-up car stereos was just an ordinary part of their lives. If their existing stereo broke down they would simply make inquiries about the availability of another, steal one or have someone steal it for them:

> *In that car I had six or seven stereos. Some I nicked and some I asked people to get for me. I had a really good stereo in it and then the electrics went on it. So I asked someone to go and get me one, because I didn't really like to go out and do it because I had moved on from car stereos. That was a little boys' thing. I asked some little guy over there [points to block of flats] to go and get me one. It took three days for him to get the stereo. I asked him to get me a high quality one and he came back with a Sony, a big face on it like - one of the top Sony ones.*

Cheques and credit cards

The 1996 BCS found that one in 10 car thefts involved theft of bags or purses. It also found that eight percent of BCS respondents had been mugged in the past year; many of these victims would have had their purses and wallets stolen. The BCS also found that seven percent of burglary victims had credit cards stolen and four percent had cheque books stolen. Research by Levi et al (1991) looked at a sample of Barclaycards that had been stolen and found the average loss to be £615.

Burglars and other thieves interviewed in this study regularly referred to the use of stolen cheque books and credit cards as 'kiting'.[67] Although they were not specifically asked about cheque books and credit cards, nine of those interviewed said that they had either stolen or bought and used them fraudulently to obtain goods. They also described techniques for removing signatures from stolen credit and cheque cards and other ways to make buying goods easier. Further information was given about how they were sold to dealers or handed over to specialists in kiting.

If burglars and other thieves did not sell stolen cheque books and credit cards, then kiting was something they more usually arranged for someone else to do. A heroin user, who had specialised in picking pockets, said that although he did not like kiting, he would sometimes do it because he could get far more money that way (as opposed to merely selling the cheque books and cards). However, the risks are high. One of the more experienced burglars described how he was caught and received an 18-month prison sentence for obtaining goods with cheque books he had taken during burglaries. Two plain clothes detectives followed him and arrested him, but not before he had been on many spending sprees:

> *I got arrested because I'd started doing 'kiting'. I was living with this woman and she taught me how to kite and everything [explains chemicals and technique used to remove signatures from credit cards]. She was selling them at first. Then we started buying clothes, but we'd give it up at £400. Then we'd sell the book even though that's a bit naughty 'cause you're supposed to sell it as soon as you get it... I started going on to jewellers' to buy things. Buying clothes. I did buy a heck of a lot of clothes. I had a rack of coats and loads of shoes.*

Kiting cheques and credit cards is particularly risky. Many burglars said they were reluctant to do it. Burglars caught with stolen cheque books and credit cards can be quickly and easily connected with their victims. Inexperienced burglars and thieves sometimes threw cheque books and credit cards away. They were afraid that cheque books would be too incriminating. More experienced burglars felt the same way, but had buyers for them and sold them quickly.

The most experienced burglar in this study was interviewed at the start of a nine-year sentence for aggravated burglary. When inside a dwelling he always took handbags and cash. He buried the handbags, then sold any cheques and credit cards, which he described as "...a passport to being caught." Other convicted burglars sold them for the same reason:

---

67   Defn. (Collins English Dictionary): To issue fictitious papers to obtain credit or money.

You sell them. A card for twenty five pounds. Then that person goes out and does some shopping. It's just up to the person who's buying the cheque book. Say they wanted one cheque book with quite a few cheques in it. They'd give me twenty five pounds for it. Or if he come up to me, and it was a desperate bloke, and he wanted a cheque book for fifty quid - I'd give it to him...they're no good to me 'cause I can't forge cheques.

Where stolen cheque books belong to women it is necessary to employ females to do the kiting. One heroin user described how he would go shopping with a woman to whom he would give every fourth cheque to spend on herself. Another offender from the YOI sample explained how a cheque book and card stolen from a house was 'safe' enough to use because the owners were away on holiday:

We got a cheque book and card out. We got some girl to work it for us. And we worked three grand off the cheque book and card. See, 'cause they was on holiday and it couldn't get reported stolen. We worked off three thousand pounds in clothes and jewellery and that. Me and my brother and this girl. And like, just whatever she wanted in the shops she'd buy for herself and that.

Despite the risks, heroin users were regularly involved in kiting:

I would go to my dealer and say: "I've got a cheque book, is there anything you want?" That's when I used to get big lists. Food shopping was a favourite. Going to do them say 60 quids' worth of shopping for 30 quid. Washing powder, all the dear expensive goods.

These shopping lists were mentioned by other female addicts. If they had stolen cheque books and credit cards they would buy items to order so that there was no need to find a buyer. One of the male heroin users explained how stolen cheques and credit cards were converted into valuable goods:

It usually happens in a drug den, where drugs are sold. It would be perhaps a squatted house or a squatted flat - very rarely would anyone live there. There would always be about half a dozen people selling drugs. Half a dozen people hanging about waiting for someone to come if they didn't have enough money, or beg enough money from someone to buy... They would take waist measurements, for items of clothing, jeans, trainers, jackets, everything possible, microwaves, the whole works. And then they would go with the credit cards. It was usually the women who buy the items that were required and then come back to the drug den the following day and sell them on.

Another female heroin user explained that many people dealt with the possibility that the cards might have been reported stolen by telephoning the credit card companies - pretending they owned shops and that someone had brought it into their shop to make a purchase. In that way they immediately established if the card was 'safe' to use. Another female heroin addict and drug-dealer, interviewed in Liverpool, said that in the past she had gone to off-licence shops which did not have sophisticated 'point-of-sale' terminals to check for illegal transactions (see Levi et al 1991) and made purchases for less than £30 or £40 with stolen credit cards. She bought bottles of expensive whisky which she would then sell for half price. For purchases at this level she said that the shop staff would not check if the card was stolen.[68] She was eventually caught in an off-licence when a member of staff tipped off the police, and was serving two years' probation supervision for this offence at the time of the interview.

Jewellery

Jewellery and cash were the items most sought after by those who burgled people's homes.[69] Jewellery, particularly gold, was seen as the easiest item to convert into cash.

Two burglars had sold jewellery to their normal Residential fence. Two others had, only occasionally, sold to friends. All the other burglars sold jewellery to shops that advertised their willingness to buy scrap and second-hand jewellery. The following conveys how easy it is for burglars to get immediate cash for stolen jewellery:

> *I'd seen a diamond ring before, but I'd been selling things like that for fifteen to twenty pounds or something. I didn't have a clue. But I took this one ring to this place in [name of town] and straightaway I said to the bloke "What will you give me for this?" "Well," he said, "I'll have to take the stones out and then tell you what I'll give you." He took the stones out and said, "I'll give you seventy pound for the gold and three hundred pounds for each of the three diamonds." And when it came to nine hundred and something pounds, and I didn't expect more than a hundred and fifty pounds, I thought "yep this is definitely the place to be coming."*

Another burglar said:

---

68 Known in the banking industry as a 'floor limit'. Below these limits no authorisation for transactions is required (see Levi et al 1991).

69 The 1996 BCS found that 36 percent of burglary victims (who actually had something stolen) had jewellery stolen (Mirrlees-Black et al 1996).

A lot of people who use drugs use these places, so really you got a front here to say they're buying jewellery when they're scrap metal [jewellers buying gold] and they don't know where it comes from. You go there with the stuff and you sort of get on friendly terms with someone... they just take the stones out and weigh the scrap metal. They tell you how many grams it comes to and they give you the price. ...once or twice I've been to high street shops where they've got all the jewellery in the window. I sold a chain and a couple of rings. There was a sign outside - nine carat gold for scrap or something. I gave them the jewellery. They gave me a price. I filled out a receipt in a false name and that was it.

It is not possible to gauge from this research the extent to which stolen jewellery is being sold on by jewellers to innocent consumers. While a few thieves said they knew that stolen gold and silver jewellery was being scrapped by their fence, most were not sure what the fence was doing with it.

Summary and Conclusions

Those who installed stolen car stereo equipment in their own cars would regularly take it out to 'trade-up'. The older stolen stereo would then be sold-on to friends, even for a small profit. In this way, many stolen stereos take a long time to 'end up' anywhere because they are frequently on their way to somewhere else.

Many thieves were quite prepared to steal cheque books and credit cards whenever the opportunity arose. They frequently sold these to drug users who then used money from goods bought through kiting to buy illegal drugs (see also Levi et al 1991: 5).

Burglars who were regularly using heroin or cocaine were dealing in relatively large volumes of stolen jewellery and so needed to develop special relationships with jewellers. They needed to know where it would be safe to sell regularly so they would not have to travel around looking for likely shops. Stolen jewellery, therefore, was nearly always sold by thieves in Commercial Fence Supplies markets. Once they were trusted by the jeweller there was no longer a need to fabricate a story.

Car stereo thieves are obviously attracted by the presence of expensive and superior stereos in cars. The relative ease with which they can be stolen is compounded by the readiness of others to buy, even when they already own a legitimate or stolen stereo. As many car stereos are sold through network sales, crime prevention schemes aimed at reducing these markets may have an impact on reducing thefts from cars and this is discussed further in Chapter 9.

One major concern is that expensive stereos are distinctive status symbols. The best stereos can be easily identified by looking into a car, or simply because certain makes and models of car are known to have particular stereos fitted as standard equipment (BMWs and Volkswagen Golf GTIs were commonly mentioned). Encouraging manufacturers to be less predictable in the type of equipment they fit in their cars and making it harder to tell the difference between top of the range and basic equipment, or new models from earlier versions, could have considerable pay-offs for reducing car stereo thefts - by making it more difficult for distributors to be sure that the rewards are worth the risks involved in stealing. This would also reduce consumer's confidence that they are getting a 'bargain' that they could not otherwise afford. For this to work, however, it would be necessary to replace manufacturers' existing emphasis on visible exclusivity with a new emphasis on being able to retain ownership by not flaunting it openly.

The same principle could be applied to other electrical goods including television, hi-fi and computer equipment. In the case of VCRs, simply abandoning the use of nicam stereo badges might discourage theft. The deterrent effect of existing theft resistant car stereo systems is also discussed in the next chapter.

8 CRIME PREVENTION METHODS

Before moving on to the main findings and conclusions in this report it is worth considering what thieves said about crime prevention measures. This chapter also describes how stolen goods are concealed when they are carried outside victims' homes and looks at what could be done to curtail a method burglars commonly use to decide which homes to break into.

Property marking

Property marking usually involves marking goods such as televisions, VCRs or hi-fi equipment with the owner's postcode - either visibly or invisibly. This aims to protect items from theft, or to ensure their return if recovered by the police.

When asked if they would steal items which they knew had been marked, most who had been involved in burglary said that they would (see also Knutsson 1984). Even so-called 'invisible' ultraviolet pen marks could be seen and wiped off with detergent. Engraved property marks were scratched out and 'indelible' pen marks were removed by using washing-up liquid and a scourer or a Brillo pad. Residential fences who spotted property marks would ask the thief to remove them and provide the materials to do so. Fences sometimes asked for gold jewellery to be cut up by the thief, or for jewellery marks to be removed with sand-paper before bringing it to the shop. Manufacturers' serial marks were often removed and even serial numbers on motorbikes and cars were removed by the thief once inside scrap yards. Engraved goods were pawned at pawn shops where they never asked about the marks. Fences who bought stolen computers would replace the whole of the external casing. Security tags on clothing stolen during ram raids were removed by using magnets, forks or smashing against walls.

None of those who spoke about marked property said that they were put off by it, although one of these had stolen marked property, and removed the marks, but felt that the risk of transporting marked goods was too great. Two others had never seen marked property, even though they had regularly handled stolen goods.

One interviewee had bought a stolen hi-fi and then marked it with his own pen to make it look like his own. Another bought a property-marked hi-fi system while being looked after in a local authority care home and this led to his arrest:

> *I paid for it and took it back to my room and checked it out. There was infrared pen marking all over it and I knew it was stolen because it had this bloke's name and address on it. I tried scrubbing it off. I just left it for a while and a member of staff found it in my room and they phoned the police.*

Research in Sweden to evaluate a property marking programme (Knutsson 1984) concluded that this does not provide a guarantee against loss since:

> *...numerous things are stolen although they are marked. And the probability of recovering a marked item is small...the conclusion from the study is that the actual theory underlying Operation Identification is reasonable but that reality turns out to be other than the theory assumes.*

Property marking does not appear to be a particularly effective deterrent to thieves and buyers. However, it may increase detection rates if police officers can intercept goods before they have been delivered to a fence. More research is needed to determine the effect of property marking on thieves' decision-making and to find out precisely how (Pawson and Tilley 1994) property marking may reduce theft.

Target hardening

Alarms and locks on cars and houses did not always deter because windows could be easily broken to gain entry and seize goods. Indeed, a car, house or shop alarm might go off but it does not physically prevent items from being stolen because the windows can always be broken and items removed in a matter of seconds. Good locks, by contrast, prevented highly motivated thieves who were stealing to order from getting the mountain bikes they wanted. One thief who had been stealing expensive mountain bikes to order said that it was the use of tougher mountain bike locks which led to him switching from being a bike thief to becoming a house burglar. It seems that good locks and enclosures are the most effective target hardening method where entry cannot be achieved by breaking glass. Those who stole car stereos to order said that car security systems were no deterrent because they would just break the window and steal the radio while the alarm was going off:

If it's during the day and sometimes like I don't give a shit and I want a cassette and I've been walking about looking for a cassette all day, I'll just pop the window and the alarm's going off and I'll just lean in there and get it while the alarm's going off.

By contrast, one of the interviewees explained how the use of reinforced locks had put an end to regular thefts of tools. In this case, locks which were previously accessible to bolt cutters had been modified with a strong metal shield:

Four or five years ago the thing used to be, you know those big metal containers that they leave at the side of the road, what workmen have, that they've got all the power saws and generators and everything. That used to be what we used to do. You see them everywhere. If they're doing road works somewhere. My friend's dad used to sell everything we used to get. We used to get 40 to 50 pound for the power saws. And generators were 90 to 100 pound each.

We used to go to places like Glossop, you know places out of the way, and places up near the moors. You know like quiet country villages. We used to go looking for them in a car with a pair of bolt crops. And then they used to be easy to get into but they've changed them and that's why people have stopped doing them now. They started putting square boxes over the padlock, so you couldn't get the bolt crops onto the padlock. As soon as they started doing that we just lost interest. There's just no point in staying there trying to do it.

Somewhat ironically, car stereos with in-built anti-theft features are highly prized by thieves because they command the best prices. Stereos which slide out of a car leaving a backing tray behind and those with a clip-off face were repeatedly described as the best. Cars were often broken into with the hope (frequently realised) that removable stereos were hidden under a seat or in the boot:

...you can see a slide there and the cassette's been pulled out, but people put it under the seat. But I know when I look and I'll look under the seat - or he could have put it in the glove compartment. Like if, in the night, I see a car with only the slide in I'll still pop the

*window and look in and I'll find it in the glove compartment, or in
the boot - nine times out of ten.*

This type of stereo is probably more appealing for a number of reasons. They
are invariably of better quality and were described as being stylish. It is
possible to speculate that perhaps the main reason they were preferred is
because illicit buyers were only too aware that such equipment could be
stolen and they intended always to take the removable components with
them when they parked their own cars.

Even car stereos that required a secret code number to be re-entered when
the power supply was removed were stolen:

*Even coded ones I'd have. You can get the codes taken off them for
a tenner. Places advertise in the papers. All you've got to do is say
you've forgotten your number. The person that buys it would do it
really. All they do is wipe the chip out - wipe the code chip.*

General crime prevention

In addition to supplying information about the way stolen goods markets
operate, interviewees also mentioned other facts about the 'burglary
business'. Two in particular do not appear to have been given much
coverage in the literature: the way stolen goods are concealed when carried
outside victims' homes; and the fact that most burglars use a technique
known as 'sounding the drum'.

Sounding the drum

All of the burglars interviewed said that they would use a method known as
'sounding the drum' to establish that no one was at home before attempting
to burgle a house or flat (see also Nee and Taylor 1988; Cromwell et al
1991). This technique simply involves knocking on the door or sounding the
doorbell. If someone answers, the burglar invariably seeks to avoid suspicion
by asking whether a certain person lives there or if the occupant knows
where they live. The thwarted burglar then moves on to do the same again,
in search of a property where nobody is at home. This is such a common
modus operandi that it might be worth piloting a scheme where
householders are asked to report immediately such callers via a special
police 'hotline'.

Black plastic bin bags

Burglars do not generally carry holdalls when they go stealing. Many of those interviewed used black plastic bin bags found in the properties they burgled, or pillow cases and sheets, to conceal stolen goods before they carried them outside. It is worth highlighting this fact and encouraging members of the public to be suspicious of anyone carrying items wrapped in this way around their neighbourhood. If strangers are carrying goods into taxis in this way people should be particularly suspicious.

Supply and demand

The BCS revealed that a large number of people are offered as well as buy stolen goods. Those living in poorer areas are more likely to be offered stolen goods and buy them, and many more believe that their neighbours own stolen goods.

The existence of a causal relationship between the demand for stolen goods and their supply makes intuitive sense because personal possessions are always at risk of being stolen when thieves know or believe other people will buy them (Tremblay et al 1994). However, the relationship between the willingness of individuals to buy stolen goods and the readiness of others to steal them is complex (Ferman et al 1987), and it is difficult to determine the degree to which thieves cultivate a market for things they have stolen and to what extent their offending is stimulated by the existence of ready markets. Sometimes thieves steal to order, but issues of demand and supply are not always this simple. For example, small business owners are frequently offered stolen goods by people they have never met before. This happens for two main reasons: firstly, because they are likely to have money available, and secondly, thieves simply believe that by virtue of being in business these people will buy goods from them at bargain prices. And many of them do buy. Those who have never bought stolen goods before also receive offers through hawking markets and network sales. Consequently, markets for stolen goods should be seen as both a downstream consequence of theft and also as an underlying motivational force for much acquisitive offending.

Suppliers and tradesmen

Because some electrical goods suppliers use thieves to steal expensive equipment back from their own customers, it might be worth considering setting up a pilot scheme whereby police record where victims bought any recently purchased products that have been stolen from them. This information could then be routinely analysed (Frisbie 1982; Ekblom 1988) to check for a correlation between particular suppliers and victims. Similarly, in the light of findings from other studies of burglars (Cromwell et al 1991; Wright and Decker 1994), which revealed that some tradesmen or employees of utility companies tip-off burglars or commit burglaries themselves, police officers could also collect and analyse information about recent visitors to burgled homes and office premises.

9 The Market Reduction Approach

This chapter discusses the use of a Market Reduction Approach to tackle stolen goods markets.

The situational crime prevention approach has been at the centre of crime prevention activity for many years and could be used to tackle theft by reducing stolen goods markets. It was first proposed in the Home Office publication *Crime as Opportunity* (Mayhew et al 1976) and addresses crime from the perspective of human situations and opportunities (Felson, 1994). The approach is particularly useful for designing solutions to prevent specific crime problems in the places where they usually happen.

Initiatives to reduce stolen goods markets might employ one or more of the three broad categories of situational crime prevention (Clarke 1983): those which increase the *effort* of offending; those which increase the *risk* of offending and those which reduce the *rewards* of offending. These would seek to make it more difficult for thieves to sell and to increase the real or perceived likelihood that they will be reported to the police, apprehended and/or convicted. It would also reduce rewards by either lowering the price of stolen goods or reducing the volume of sales. Initiatives might include: formal surveillance by police in Commercial Fence Supplies Markets; surveillance by employees in large companies where other employees are engaged in network sales and stealing to order; surveillance of Residential fences by residents on housing estates and 'natural surveillance' of thieves hawking stolen goods.

Individual situational crime prevention schemes will need to be tailored to particular types of market. Although it is beyond the scope of this report to present fully detailed strategies, a number of preliminary suggestions are outlined below.

Commercial Fence Supplies Markets

Investigation and preventative efforts in Commercial Fence Supplies Markets should focus on distributors - i.e. thieves and fences - because there are no consumers in these markets. At a local level, perhaps one way to reduce stolen goods markets would be to install cctv cameras (or use existing ones) to monitor whether particular suspected thieves are frequently entering certain shops (see also Kock et al 1996).

If stricter controls were imposed on crime promoters, such as businessmen who buy stolen goods, both they and the thieves who supply them would need to invest more effort in order to convert stolen property into cash. This could be achieved through imposing statutory, or encouraging voluntary, obligations on shopkeepers and other businessmen, particularly car breakers, to conduct transactions with members of the public 'on camera', or to require that all sellers are photographed. Stricter requirements of proof of ownership might also be considered.

Taken alone it is unlikely that these measures would have any significant impact, as transactions would simply become more secretive. However, as part of a wider and co-ordinated operation aimed at market reduction they would send a clear message to thieves and handlers that their activities were becoming more risky and perhaps, for many, no longer worth that risk.

Commercial Sales Markets

These usually involve members of the public as innocent consumers. Therefore, crime prevention schemes should concentrate upon distributors. Increased formal surveillance would increase the risks involved in stealing - since being caught trying to sell stolen goods would make it easier for the police to connect the seller with the theft.

Other measures to reduce the rewards of offending might include 'removing inducements'. For example, shops dealing in second-hand goods (including jewellers) could be required or encouraged to display signs that send out a clear message that they are enrolled in a crime prevention programme aimed at preventing theft and handling stolen goods. This would also have an added effect of increasing the perceived risk of selling. Property marking schemes, which engrave electrical goods with the owner's name and address, might also be effective because they would reduce the second-hand value of goods. Deeply engraving "NOT FOR RESALE" in very large letters, along with the telephone number of a 'hotline' for reporting suspected stolen goods, might be particularly effective. Such marks are much harder to remove than visible and 'invisible' property marks made with a marker pen, and any attempts to do so would be likely to reduce considerably the value of goods. However, low 'take-up' of property marking schemes has always been a problem, and is likely to be greater in areas where residents have stolen goods in their homes. Indeed, for males in the 1994 BCS, aged 36-60, not having security marked property was one of four variables significantly associated with buying stolen goods. The other three variables were all indicators of living in a poor area and financial hardship.

Hawking Markets

Consumers may be 'innocent' when they buy in Commercial Sales Markets, but they are not so 'innocent' when they buy stolen goods in pubs or at their doorstep. In addition to the surveillance measures described above, it might be worth piloting (and evaluating) a scheme to increase awareness of the consequences of buying stolen goods. Recent 'Don't drink and drive' public information campaigns have been credited with considerable success in reducing alcohol related car crashes. Something similar might emphasise the deleterious effects of buying stolen goods. However, as Graham and Bennett (1995) point out '...care needs to be taken in the planning of publicity campaigns to ensure that they do not inadvertently increase fear of crime and/or lead to over-reaction.' There is also the possibility that publicity campaigns might even raise awareness of the potential to buy desirable consumer goods cheaply.

Network Sales

It might also be worth piloting 'Rule Setting' schemes to remove any ambiguity in what is and is not acceptable behaviour (see Graham and Bennett 1995). Through tackling specific illegal trading subcultures in specific locations, potential consumers in network sales might be dissuaded from buying. Publicity campaigns could be used to discourage people from buying stolen goods and encourage them to report those who do. Campaigns could emphasise that stealing to order markets thrive within network sales and clearly stimulate more *supply by theft*.

Residential Fence Supplies

More police resources could be focused on identifying and arresting Residential fences. Only two of the interviewees knew of Residential fences who had been arrested and imprisoned for handling stolen goods. However, both said this knowledge had significantly reduced their own offending because they were afraid that the police would also learn about them. In one case, a young woman said she had stopped buying and selling stolen goods permanently when a local Residential fence was arrested. In another case, a young burglar explained how he stopped offending for over a year when he was 16 because his local Residential fence had been arrested:

> *That was a shock to me when my friend told me that he had been arrested. I just kept it down because I knew if he said something they [the police] would come straight at me.*

In both of these cases the interviewees were not offending to finance drug use and were only offending on a monthly basis. It seems unlikely that more experienced or prolific distributors of stolen goods would reduce their offending so dramatically - particularly if they were using theft to finance illegal drug use. However, Edmunds et al (1996) suggest that law enforcement can disrupt illicit drugs markets and that novice users may well be deterred from buying.

Reducing drug markets is likely to reduce the overall incidence of crime because acquisitive crime is commonly used to fund drug abuse (Jochelson 1995, Edmunds et al 1996). Therefore, it might be worth developing a strategy which combines efforts to reduce illicit drug markets with schemes aimed at reducing stolen goods markets. Such an approach would tackle two of the principal causes of serious theft.

Displacement

One criticism commonly levelled against the situational crime prevention approach is that it simply displaces crime to another relatively 'safer' place or time. Offenders may change their method of offending, choosing different targets (e.g. stealing cash and credit cards rather than goods), or new offenders may emerge who are not deterred (Bennett and Wright 1984; Barr and Pease 1990; Wright and Decker 1994).

The greatest success in limiting displacement from hardened targets to those which are relatively more vulnerable occurs when a whole class of potential targets are simultaneously protected (Graham and Bennett 1995), or when adequately funded target hardening and other situational measures are combined with community-oriented action (Ekblom et al, 1996). Therefore, to prevent thieves switching to different types of theft and different markets, a particularly suitable approach would involve simultaneously tackling all types of stolen goods market at the local area level. Linking public awareness campaigns and community action with police operations, and situational measures, a Market Reduction Approach would aim to reduce the ability of thieves to cultivate new outlets and also disrupt existing illegal trading. The main objective would be a general reduction of acquisitive crime levels. The most desirable outcome would involve offenders exploring non-criminal alternatives, rather than just alternative crimes. As Clarke (1995) points out:

Under the rational choice assumptions that now guide thinking about situational prevention, displacement is no longer seen as inevitable but as contingent on the offenders' judgements about the ease, risks, and attractiveness of alternative crimes.

A Broad Strategy

Tackling acquisitive crime in this way might also satisfy the demands of crime prevention professionals seeking to 'tackle the whole picture by treating crime problems with a broader brush' - to deal with the underlying causes of criminal motivation as well as the vulnerability of victims' possessions (Sutton 1996). The Market Reduction Approach might also allay criticisms aimed at the so called 'siege mentality' of the Situational Crime Prevention Approach (Tilley 1992), when used in 'lock it or lose it' style crime prevention programmes, which appear to blame victims for not 'properly' securing their belongings more than they blame the thieves. In addition to using situational crime prevention methods to reduce stolen goods markets, at a wider level the Market Reduction Approach could involve new ways to make certain luxury goods affordable legitimately for low income groups. This might be achieved by encouraging manufacturers to lower initial prices of new technology through prolonging the period over which they seek to recover their investment. As part of a long-term strategy it might even be worth considering tax breaks on such products.

Overall, we should seek to price offenders out of the market, ideally as part of a broader strategic movement (Clarke, 1995; Ekblom, 1997). Towards this goal, the Market Reduction Approach provides a new route for utilising the effectiveness of situational crime prevention. It addresses an important underlying 'social cause' of theft while employing an existing approach with a good pedigree, proven to prevent crimes in places where they usually happen.

APPENDIX I

The logistic regression models and supplementary tables

The variables included in the two models summarised in Tables 3.3 and 5.3 are set out below (Figs A1.1 and A1.2). Logistic regression, or Logit, is a statistical technique which can be used to measure the strength of relationships between predictor (independent) variables (e.g. age, gender and type of neighbourhood) and outcome (dependent) variables: i.e. *buying stolen goods*. It also shows the influence of each predictor variable on the likelihood of the outcome variable taking place. Highly correlated variables can cause effects in logistic regression which are difficult to interpret. Therefore, variables to be entered into each model were placed into a correlation matrix. No two variables had a correlation coefficient greater than 0.5. These figures show the estimated coefficients for the independent (predictor) variables and the 'main effects' details (in these models, interactions between predictor variables were not examined).

All independent variables were dichotomised (coded 1 for present and 0 for absent). The coefficients represent the amount of change in the outcome variable (e.g. buying stolen goods) when the explanatory variable in the model is present (e.g. respondent being male) as opposed to absent (e.g. respondent being female). The data set was not weighted and the main BCS weighting variables (number of adults in the household and whether or not the respondent lived in an inner city area) were entered in the model to see if they were significant.

The sign of significant coefficients indicates the direction in which the predictor lays. Turning to the first model by way of example (buying stolen goods - Fig A1.1), respondents in Age (1) were more likely to have bought stolen goods than those aged 36 to 60, which is the reference category. This is not displayed because the reference categories in logistic regression models are necessarily nil (Norusis, 1990).

As outlined in Chapter 3, the risk scale used was generated from responses to questions concerning drug use, going out behaviour and heavy drinking. One point was added to each respondent's risk-score for each additional component of risky behaviour. The categories in the model are for those with four to eight points (high risk) compared with no more than one point (low risk) and those with two or three points (medium risk). The coefficients in the model are based on the probability of respondents in the high risk category buying stolen goods compared with those in the low to medium risk (combined) categories. Coefficients for the Acorn groups displayed in the models are based on the probability of respondents in each group buying stolen goods compared with those in Acorn group A (thriving) which is not displayed. (For a more detailed yet straightforward explanation of how to interpret such models, see Lloyd, et al 1994.)

To arrive at the final models for buying and being offered stolen goods, 30 variables were entered into each model one-by-one. This method is known as Forward Stepwise entry and is described in detail in Norusis (1990: p 66). The following 30 variables were initially entered into the models:

Attitudinal variables: Drug problem in area; satisfaction with neighbourhood; whether socially cohesive neighbourhood; levels of friendship and acquaintances in neighbourhood; measure of difficulty in recognising strangers in the neighbourhood; belief in likelihood of being burgled in next 12 months; belief that most burglaries in the area are committed by locals; whether burglar alarms and other security devices actually make homes safer in area; whether street robbery is a problem in the area; whether household property is security marked.

Demographic and other background variables: lost wage in household; whether respondent is managing on income; family structure; inner city area; gender; age; ACORN classification; burgled in past 12 months; whether respondent is head of the household; whether head of household is self-employed; interviewers assessment of physical state of homes in neighbourhood; type of accommodation in which respondent lives (flat, semi-detached, detached etc); whether household has use of a car; total household income; risk variable (based on lifestyle factors); carried more than £200 outside of home in past month; member of neighbourhood watch group; whether house is alarmed; whether household insured against property theft; number of years lived in area; whether they know anyone who has been burgled in past year.

In effect, each variable entered in the model is tested for possible removal on the basis of the significance level of the Wald statistic (Figs A1.1, A1.2).

Tables A1.4, A1.5, A1.6 and A1.7 also display the B and R statistics. Graham and Bowling (1995) explain how to interpret the B coefficient and the R statistic. The R statistic is used to look at the strength of association between the dependent variable and each of the independent variables[70]. R can range in value from -1 to +1. A positive value indicates that as the variable increases in value so does the likelihood of an event occurring. If R is negative the opposite is true. Small values for R indicate that the variable makes only a small contribution to the model.

Table A1.1 Buying stolen goods

	Chi-Square	df	Significance
-2 Log Likelihood	2575.476	3827	0.0000
Model Chi-Square	303.043	14	0.0000
Improvement	7.874	2	0.0195
Goodness of Fit	3732.987	3827	0.0000

Variables in the Equation							
Variable	B	S.E.	Wald	df	Sig	R	Exp(B)
DRUGS	0.2799	0.1127	6.1726	1	0.0130	0.0381	1.3231
LOSTWAGE	0.3458	0.1340	6.6573	1	0.0099	0.0402	1.4131
NOTMANGE	0.4212	0.1128	13.9346	1	0.0002	0.0644	1.5238
ACORNGR			7.2914	2	0.0261	0.0338	
(1)	0.5140	0.1930	7.0950	1	0.0077	0.0421	1.6720
(2)	0.4375	0.1812	5.8307	1	0.0157	0.0365	1.5488
HHSELF	0.3989	0.1638	5.9329	1	0.0149	0.0370	1.4902
HHCAR	0.3140	0.1354	5.3750	1	0.0204	0.0342	1.3688
LESSCASH	0.4114	0.1129	13.2796	1	0.0003	0.0626	1.5090
LOCALBUR	0.3177	0.1076	8.7121	1	0.0032	0.0483	1.3740
HIRISK	0.2956	0.1097	7.2550	1	0.0071	0.0427	1.3439
AGE			103.5982	2	0.0000	0.1860	
(1)	1.4149	0.1414	100.1566	1	0.0000	0.1847	4.1160
(2)	0.8601	0.1240	48.1331	1	0.0000	0.1266	2.3633
SEX	0.4779	0.1095	19.0439	1	0.0000	0.0769	1.6126
NORANCE	0.2720	0.1318	4.2606	1	0.0390	0.0280	1.3126
Constant	-4.2124	0.2113	397.5035	1	0.0000		

---

70   This statistic is directly analogous to the correlation coefficient Pearson's R, except that it takes into account the effects of other relevant variables.

71   The English survey combined buying and selling stolen goods as one question and is excluded from this analysis.

Table A1.2 Offered stolen goods

	Chi-Square	df	Significance
-2 Log Likelihood	2432.033	3829	0.0000
Model Chi-Square	454.300	12	0.0000
Improvement	6.436	1	0.0112
Goodness of Fit	3724.157	3829	0.0000

Variable	B	S.E.	Wald	df	Sig	R	Exp(B)
NEIGHBS	0.9447	0.1780	28.1609	1	0.0000	0.0952	2.5720
DRUGS	0.4953	0.1124	19.4141	1	0.0000	0.0777	1.6410
NOTMANGE	0.2766	0.1092	6.4123	1	0.0113	0.0391	1.3186
ACORNGR			11.2915	2	0.0035	0.0503	
(1)	0.6219	0.1892	10.8049	1	0.0010	0.0552	1.8624
(2)	0.4056	0.1809	5.0243	1	0.0250	0.0324	1.5001
LESSCASH	0.5513	0.1126	23.9781	1	0.0000	0.0873	1.7354
DIFSTRAN	0.2735	0.1066	6.5788	1	0.0103	0.0398	1.3146
HIRISK	0.3677	0.1125	10.6747	1	0.0011	0.0548	1.4444
AGE			160.0871	2	0.0000	0.2325	
(1)	1.7919	0.1422	158.8196	1	0.0000	0.2331	6.0010
(2)	0.7601	0.1289	34.7561	1	0.0000	0.1065	2.1386
SEX	0.7150	0.1128	40.1992	1	0.0000	0.1150	2.0443
BURGLARY	0.6074	0.1121	029.3474	1	0.0000	0.0973	1.8356
Cons	-5.4357	0.2747	391.5396	1	0.0000		

Supplementary Table

Table A1.3 Reasons for not having household contents insured against theft by purchasing stolen goods

	too expensive		prop not at risk		insurance refused		not got around to renewing		can't be bothered		other/ D/know	
		%		%		%		%		%		%
Bought stolen goods												
Yes	91	22	8	26	5	32	26	14	12	28	11	14
No	332	78	33	74	9	68	139	86	28	72	76	86

Follow-up sample A, those without insurance against theft. Weighted data, unweighted N.

Table A1.4 Buyers of Stolen Goods: Males and Females

Variable	B	s.s	odds ratio	R
Drugs problem in neighbourhood	0.2799	**	1.3	0.38
Recent loss of wage earner in household	0.3458	**	1.4	0.40
Not managing very well on income	0.4212	***	1.5	0.64
ACORN GROUP †				
Rising/Striving	0.5140	**	1.6	0.04
Expanding/Settling/Aspiring	0.4375	*	1.5	0.03
Head of household self-employed	0.3989	*	1.4	0.37
Household without use of a car	0.3140	*	1.3	0.03
Carried more than £200 of cash in the past month	0.4114	**	1.5	0.06
Believe most burglaries in area committed by locals	0.3177	**	1.3	0.04
High Risk Score	0.2956	**	1.3	0.42
AGE ‡				
16 - 24	1.4149	****	4.1	0.18
25 - 35	0.8601	****	2.3	0.12
Being Male	0.4779	****	1.6	0.07
No household contents insurance	0.2720	*	1.3	0.02

s.s *p<0.05 **p<0.01 ***p<0.001 ****P<0.0001
Unweighted data. Source:1994 BCS. Follow-up A sample.
† Estimate of the increased odds of buying stolen goods are compared with Acorn group: *Thriving*
‡ Estimate of the increased odds of buying stolen goods are compared with Age group 36-60

Table A1.5 Buying Stolen Goods: males

Variable	B	s.s	odds ratio	R
Drugs problem in neighbourhood	0.3967	**	1.4	0.05
Not managing very well on income	0.6670	****	1.9	0.11
ACORN GROUP †				
Rising/Striving	0.6181	*	1.8	0.49
Expanding/Settling/Aspiring	0.6004	*	1.8	0.05
Head of household self-employed	0.5508	*	1.7	0.03
Interviewers assessment of physical state of homes in neighbourhood as mainly bad or very bad ‡	0.8182	*	2.2	0.05
Carried more than £200 of cash in the past month	0.4410	**	1.5	0.06
AGE §				
16 - 17	1.6308	****	5.1	0.11
18 - 21	1.9480	****	7.0	0.19
22 - 25	1.5478	****	4.7	0.17
26 - 30	0.9460	****	2.5	0.11
31 - 36	0.7377	***	2.0	0.08

s.s *p<0.05 **p<0.01 ***p<0.001 ****P<0.0001
Unweighted data. Source:1994 BCS. Follow-up A sample.
† Estimate of the increased odds of buying stolen goods are compared with Acorn group: *Thriving*
‡ Estimate of the increased odds of buying stolen goods are compared with assessment of homes as mainly very good
§ Estimate of the increased odds of buying stolen goods are compared with age group 37-60.

Table A1.6 Buying Stolen Goods: females

Variable	B	s.s	odds ratio	R
Recent loss of wage earner in household	0.4640	*	1.5	0.04
Not managing very well on income	0.3569	*	1.4	0.04
Household without use of a car	0.6268	***	1.8	0.08
Carried more than £200 of cash in				
the past month	0.4172	*	1.5	0.05
Easy to recognise a stranger in neighbourhood	0.3900	*	1.4	0.05
Believe most burglaries in area committed				
by locals	0.4065	*	1.5	0.05
High Risk Score	0.5046	**	1.6	0.07
AGE †				
16 - 17	1.3419	**	3.8	0.07
18 - 21	0.9536	***	2.5	0.08
22 - 25	1.5682	****	4.7	0.17
26 - 30	1.0632	****	2.8	0.12
31 - 36	0.7510	***	2.1	0.12

s.s *p<0.05 **p<0.01 ***p<0.001 ****P<0.0001
Unweighted data. Source:1994 BCS. Follow-up A sample.
† Estimate of the increased odds of buying stolen goods are compared with Age group 37-60

Table A1.7 Offered Stolen Goods: final model

Variable	B	s.s	odds ratio	R
Believe many neighboursown stolen goods	0.9447	****	2.5	0.09
Drugs problem in neighbourhood	0.4953	****	1.6	0.77
Not managing very well on income	0.2766	**	1.3	0.03
ACORN GROUP †				
Rising/Striving	0.6219	***	1.8	0.55
Expanding/Settling/Aspiring	0.4056	*	1.5	0.32
Carried more than £200 of cash				
in the past month	0.5513	****	1.7	1.73
Easy to recognise a stranger in the				
neighbourhood	0.2735	**	1.3	0.03
High Risk Score	0.3677	***	1.4	0.05
AGE ‡				
16 - 24	1.7919	****	6.0	0.23
25 - 35	0.7601	****	2.1	0.10
Being Male	0.7150	****	2.0	0.11
Personally know someone who was				
burgled in past year	0.6074	****	1.8	0.09

s.s *p<0.05 **p<0.01 ***p<0.001 ****P<0.0001
Unweighted data. Source:1994 BCS. Follow-up A sample
† Estimate of the increased odds of being offered stolen goods are compared with Acorn group: *Thriving*
‡ Estimate of the increased odds of being offered stolen goods are compared with Age group 36-60

APPENDIX 2

The in-depth sample

The 45 in-depth interviewees were sampled from a number of sources. A number of young people who had previously taken part in the Youth Lifestyles Survey in 1993 (Graham and Bowling 1995) had given their consent to be contacted for interview in the future. Letters were sent out to 50 young people in September 1995. Many letters were returned marked "moved away". A total of 14 wrote back and agreed to be interviewed. Interviews took place either at the young person's home or (in three cases) at the Home Office. All interviews were taped and later transcribed into a thematic data set. Prior to commencing the interview, respondents were given explicit assurances of confidentiality. Many of them wanted to know precise details about how the report would be compiled and how anonymity could be ensured. They were shown a copy of an earlier Home Office research study of self-reported offending (Light et al 1993) and were relieved by the absence of names, or any other details that could be used to identify similar individuals. Interviewees were also told that if at any time they were unhappy with information they provided, the tape would be stopped and particular sections could be erased. None actually took up this offer, but it seemed to put them more at ease. In one case, it was necessary to hand the tape recorder to a more wary interviewee so that he felt in control of the interview. Following a lengthy interview with a female drug addict (heroin and cocaine), it was decided that the study should include a sample of regular heroin users to cover the particularly extensive rate of property offending among such drug users. Consequently, a sample of 10 heroin addicts (or ex-addicts) were interviewed at two separate drug-treatment clinics.

A further 10 young men were interviewed at a Young Offenders Institution. Members of the psychology department obtained consent to be interviewed of those who had particularly extensive offending histories for burglary, other thefts and car crime.

The Probation Service, in conjunction with a multi-agency crime prevention partnership, allowed us to interview six young people from a 'motor-project' who had been involved with theft from and theft of cars. The Probation Service also secured the consent of a more serious male offender with a lengthy history of car crime.

A total of four adult male prisoners were interviewed in three training prisons. The Probation Officer attached to the prisons was asked to help obtain co-operation from those with a particularly serious and lengthy history of burglary, other serious acquisitive crime, and handling stolen goods.

APPENDIX 3

"Aladdin's" Cave: A Concerted Criminal Effort

The following account was produced by Professor Mike Maguire, University of Wales. This unpublished material was used as background information for: Maguire, M. (1982). *Burglary in a Dwelling: the offence, the offender and the victim.* Heinemann, London.

X was a 60-year-old manager of a general store, with no previous convictions, who became one of the central figures in one of the biggest scale criminal organisations in Southtown for some years. For a period of at least 18 months, the rear of his shop was the depot for many of the valuable goods (particularly colour televisions and other electrical gear), stolen by the most active burglars in the town. His side of the story is that he was trapped into it by a neighbour (Y) with many criminal contacts, who sent them to him. It began "as a favour" with a single television set, but as the news spread, he found himself inundated with goods and orders, and when he tried to stop, was threatened with violence. He would pay perhaps £100 cash for a television and store it in his back room, then Y would find him a buyer and take most of the profit (sometimes, X claims, Y received the money and gave him nothing).

He described a typical transaction as follows:

"A man would come into my shop and say 'I hear you buy televisions. You're getting one tonight - we want a hundred quid for it.' Then I'd bargain him down to say £85, and that night someone else would come round in a car and I'd pay him. Then I'd tell Y about it, and he'd say 'I'll find a buyer for you.' Perhaps three days later someone else I didn't know would come and collect it, and then Y would come in a say 'Here's fifty pounds - I'll give you another fifty next week.' Sometimes I'd get the other fifty, sometimes not. I didn't know any of these people, except sometimes by first names, and I tried to stop thinking about the whole business. But it went on and on. It was a relief in many ways when the police came. I told them everything I knew, and now some of them are threatening me about what will happen when I get out of prison." (X received two years' sentence).

Some of the goods which passed through his hands finished up as far apart as Cornwall and London. From a variety of sources, I have managed to build up a picture of what happened in particular cases. For example, two burglars stole a television on the night of April 19th. That night they wrapped it in polythene and hid it in a wood. The next evening, they went to a public house and asked friends who wanted to buy one. Z showed interest, and offered them £50, to which they agreed. The next day, Z went to X and told him to expect a visitor that night. That evening he got another friend to drive the four of them out to the hiding place, dropped off the two burglars, and took the set to X's shop, collecting £80 for it. He gave the driver £5, and £50 to the burglars, whom he saw in the pub again and spent most of the £25 profit quickly on a late-night visit to a club. The next day, X saw Y, and Y set about finding a buyer. His sister and her husband from London were visiting him, and as he had already sold them a television before, he asked if anyone they knew wanted one. They said, "How much?" and he offered it for £100, to which they agreed. In this case, Y himself collected the set, and the same evening, the television was on its way to London. There, they sold it to a friend for £120, of which they sent £100 to Y a week later. He kept £15 and gave £85 to X.

Thus the set went through at least nine pairs of hands in 10 days, the "value" of the set increasing by 140 percent over the time, and the handlers collecting profit as follows:

Burglar A	£25
Burglar B	£25
Contact Z	£25
Driver	£5
X	£5
Y	£15
Y's relatives	£20

Total £120 (to which one should perhaps add the final possessor's saving of about £80 on a good second-hand colour television.)

Some idea of the scale of the 'organisation' can be gained from the following facts: £4,000 worth of property was recovered, 12 people were charged with handling stolen goods, seven with burglary of property found in the shop, and at least five others were strongly suspected of involvement, but proof was lacking. However, if one takes the word of the shop manager, there are at least 20 others he does not know whom he met personally offering him stolen goods, not to mention other minor 'cogs' such as drivers or people who stored goods for a night until it could be taken to X's shop.

But by no means everybody knew everybody else, so following all the various lines was extremely difficult for the police. The only place they could strike with certainty was in the area bounded by the 'circle' in the following diagram:

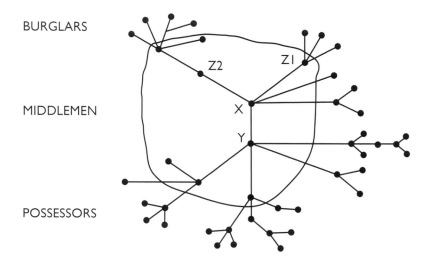

APPENDIX 4

Case studies (oral histories)

Research suggests that there is a strong link between parental criminality and criminal involvement (West 1982). Although parents of delinquents might openly condemn criminal behaviour, despite their own lawbreaking (West 1982), they might also rationalise ownership of stolen goods (Sutton 1995). Many studies have looked at the association between delinquent peers and criminality (e.g. Shaw and McKay 1942, Cohen 1955, Sarnecki 1986). The association between delinquent relatives and offending should also be explored in more depth as there may be important lessons to learn for future policy making.

Relatives were mentioned by thieves interviewed in this study on many occasions. A few parents had bought stolen goods from their children, or accepted them as presents. Uncles and aunts had bought stolen goods from their nephews and nieces and from friends of their nephews and nieces. More criminally experienced brothers and cousins had also introduced younger relatives to burglary and fencing outlets. And the most experienced and persistent burglar had been taught how to burgle by his father. The following case studies were selected from recordings of in-depth interviews with particular offenders who provided unexpectedly detailed accounts of their lives. The role that family members played in their offending was mentioned by many of those we interviewed for this study and is particularly marked in the first two of the three oral histories included here.

Adult prison [male aged 50]

I'm a burglar and middleman. I was involved in selling on loads of stuff really, but never computers. I did jewellery, bicycles …well, you name it really, I suppose…mainly antiques I was in to. I got known as a middleman basically around the time of videos being big. Before that, I'd been doing burglaries myself.

My first conviction was in 1958. I'm 50 now, and I think I was about 13 then…about12 or 13. I'd been in little bits of minor trouble then. My father would send us out to go stealing. …he gave us threats of beatings and that… we was very traumatised as kids and that. Sometimes he would come with us, cos I was only slim, only a slim chap like. My father had never been caught by the police in his whole life; well, only for motoring offences. But he was a very vicious father…he was wicked, he was striking us. He was mental in the head anyway - schizo - he had electric shock treatment, went all through that. He was a very violent man, very violent towards the family etc - to my mother especially.

There were eight of us kids in the family; I'm the second eldest. My dad used to get me and my elder brother involved in crime and stuff. I was only eight or nine years old when it started. He used to send us round to the riding stables to start with, and when all the jockeys had gone out, they'd gone out working the horses…well, we were gypsy boys really, going in nicking their wallets and that, giving them to dad…and, you know, he'd give us a pat on the back and that. We didn't want to go, we was afraid of doing it. That became a habit for many years, a good few years - into cloakrooms, changing rooms, and clubs, you know…not houses at all. It was dead easy…it was just smashing a window or something, and dad'd lift us through…I mean, we'd get in no problem. I found it quite exciting at the age of 12, 13…not so much when I was a kid getting hidings if I didn't go and do it. My mum, though, she was right against it.

We did it pretty regular, about two or three times a week. That went on since I was, say, nine, until I got Approved School for stealing. I'd been in children's homes prior to Approved School if I needed care and protection from my violent father. A few of my brothers were in homes, but the others were at home with mum. I was in children's homes for quite a long time, and then I done a length of time at Approved School, but I kept running away and that. When I actually got caught nicking, what happened was…I nicked a pay-packet out of the Master's bedroom. Well, basically then I was grassed up by some younger kids, cos I'd got more sweets and that - that was partly why I got sent to Approved School. Then all this stuff came out about a shop being robbed, and then another shop…there were a lot of grasses anyway in our little circle of children's home kids. I got Approved School for three and a half years. The shops I broke into were what you would call, well, just little small shops really, not big stores or nothing, just corner shops. I was staying in the children's home when I started breaking into shops. We'd take mainly sweets, things to eat, maybe fags, but we didn't use to take many fags. Nowadays we'd take thousands of them, but then we didn't realise the value of them. We just did it for a laugh then really. I got away with a lot. There was very little I got nicked for at that time, you know, I was lucky.

I was 15 and a half when I came out of Approved School. Then I did some farm work in Gloucester, and I was accused of thieving there, which I was, I must be honest with you. Nothing came of it cos I'd just been released from Approved School. I was put in a house there on the farm while I worked on the farm. I was nicking their little kids' money boxes and things. I knew they knew it was me, but I couldn't stop it, I just couldn't stop myself doing it basically. I'd just go into the rooms and take the money boxes or purse...

As a result I was brought back to Oxford. I was put there under a court thing. I lived there for a little bit with this private detective, and then ran away...that was cos we thought he was a bit of a perv to be honest with you, so me and this other lad run away to High Wycombe, we got caught etc. Eventually we got caught and put in a detention centre, then borstal. Basically I was thieving all the time. In between all the gaps, that's all my life has consisted of really...thieving, thieving, prison, prison, prison whatever. I don't think I've ever skipped a week of doing burglaries in my life to be honest with you - ashamed to say that.

After I left the guy who was licensed to look after me, the private detective bloke, I was still doing burglaries etc. It wasn't long before I got put away again...if you could see my record in front of me, you could see it was months, it was never years. I think the longest I've stayed out since 1958, 'til the age of 50 is 22 months, and that was a miracle, and that was only cos I didn't get caught. Most of the time I'd get caught within a few months of being out. I've been inside over 20 times...I've done Approved School, detention, borstal, borstal recall...I've done prison; six month, nine month, 12 month, 15 month, 18 month, three years, three years, three years, three years, three years, nine years, nine and a half years...I'm sure it's more than that though. I've been in prison basically all my life. I went on probation when I was 38 years of age, and I thought it was a bit late then anyway. It was just custodial, custodial from day one really.

When I broke into houses, I'd always look for money first, then jewellery, any jewellery that was going. In those days, when I was about 16, like, you didn't have to look for it; it was on the mantelpiece etc...people were much more trusting than they are today, they would just leave doors open. With jewellery, in them days, I'd just go to the old second-hand shops which were in abundance in those days, or go to a pawnbrokers - there would be no questions asked like...just be 'alright mate, how much do you want for it?' ...never no questions asked really. It was just too easy in those days.

The first thing that I bought that was stolen was videos - and I thieved them myself as well. That was basically when they first come out, shortly after, when they were very expensive...sort of late '70s, early '80s. By then, I was a fully fledged thief anyway. It was more or less the richer type of person who had the videos, hence probably the bigger houses etc, but they had more security...so, sometimes, I'd say to someone 'if you go and get us a video like, you know, I'll give you X amount of pounds for it if you do the burglary yourself.' They were more risky, in them days I found, the houses that had the videos. So they would go and do the burglary, and that'd be less risk to me. They'd come to me with the ones they'd stolen themselves, I'd make it as cheap as possible obviously. Off hand, I'd probably give them about £75 for it...probably less. I'd get double profit on it. When videos first come out, I could get, off a fence, £150, no trouble. Back then, you could sell thousands of them really. It was greed really...greed, greed, greed...got as many as I could. In a good week, I'd be getting eight to 10. Quick phone call and I'd be shifting them no problem; there was always buyers. I had people that'd ask me to get videos if I could...that's how I got into it - people'd just ask me to get them. After they first come in, the first four or five years, there was a pretty good market for them. And then, basically, the shops started selling them cheap...discounts for this and everything, even the poor could afford them really, so they're not really worth getting any more.

Sometimes the police would suspect you and they'd come round and search the house...you might be lucky and they might find nothing, and they'd say well, we're keeping an eye on you - we know you've done it but we can't prove it. It was items that they found in the house, really, anything really...like antique things; little porcelain figurines which I didn't think was worth anything, but I took them for mum; they was up on the mantelpiece. Well, it took years to find out, but he, my own father, was in with the police, he was a grass as well, behind our backs. We were still pretty naive at 15, 16, 17; even more naive when our father was telling us to go out and he'd go out with us...but he was a grass, he was grassing us kids up, cos he was an evil man. As we grew older, and he knew that we could get the better of him...he could belt us up when we was kids, but then we could get the better of him cos as we were getting older, he was getting older; he was getting older and we were getting fitter, very fit in them days. We suspected he was a grass, but we said, 'oh no, he wouldn't grass on us.' After my father had died, though, a copper told me. He told me some instances...like we'd bury stuff, not only take it indoors, but also we'd bury it under cabbages and that. We'd dig a furrow in the back garden and stick the cabbages back in...I mean, you would never know, you would never know there was stuff there...we'd even bury in deep trenches, dig a big hole for it, you know...course dad knew about all this. We often wondered...it was only when the copper said, things started coming back. Cos the police used to come round to our house and go straight out the back - not upstairs first or downstairs first as usual, it was always straight out the back. I though 'how the bloody hell did they know, they must be clever like.' I thought I'd been cleverer than them, but father was telling them all the time. Basically he was buying himself off. He did get arrested a few times on suspicion of things and they were letting him go...

I've been in shops and supermarkets, this is the gospel truth...more these days than in them days, and you get people at the checkout saying 'oh yeah, me and so and so are going on holiday soon,' like, you know. Course, my ears are tuned straight in. So, I'd get in the car and follow them out, follow them to their address. You'd get them saying 'oh the neighbours are keeping an eye on the place', but what neighbours are going to stay awake 24 hours a day? Neighbours don't really care, not really...course, if it's not alarmed, it's easy. Now I go in banks; you can see what people are drawing out and things, see what goes in the handbags. It was always handbags with me, ashamed to say it but, I know what they've got in it. Follow them home, leave it a little while, then go back. I'd come up with some excuse, like, 'oh, I'm just checking the drains outside, my love.' ... I did that for about 8-10 years.

It's more the elderly I've got into now, I'm ashamed to say it, but I must be honest with you. There's a spate of elderly people being robbed, cos I learned through experience that young witnesses sometimes make good witnesses...if young people spotted me breaking into houses, I'd get chased and everything...it's got more to the elderly now. I'm ashamed to say it, but I am what I am, and that's why I'm getting copped for bigger amounts of time.

I haven't made that much out of it in my lifetime. I mean, if I could go and start again, I wouldn't be a burglar, I wouldn't be a thief, I'd leave it alone. Generally, I'd get very little from most of the houses I burgled. With most people, it's plastic cards now, Autobanks this, all the rest of it. Very little money I have personally found about...nowadays, apart from a few good finds of jewellery and that, very little cash. I wouldn't personally hold onto stuff unless I had to. I'd try and sell it as soon as I could, like. But, you know, it there was some antique shop I thought was diddling me a bit and I knew it was worth more, cos I'd looked through the antique books, I would go and bury it. I'd rather bury it then to be honest with you. On allotments, you sometimes get the mounds of earth, you know, which people have discarded, they don't want - they've just dug their bit of allotment, leave the horrible soil, got all the lovely soil put on top. So there's big mounds of earth, pretty soft, you know, sometimes a bit tough, but I'd dig it up...put all the stinging nettles back as they should be and that - meticulous really. I'd bury it as otherwise I'd be losing my profits; that's getting desperate if you just sell it straight away. I'd try and find a good buyer, cos if you don't find a good buyer, to me personally that burglary hasn't been worth the risk.

It doesn't matter what I've got in my pocket, I'm out burgling again, no problem. I never saved any money. I know I'm evil, not as evil as the evilest people, but to rob off the elderly to me is evil. But I still feel compelled. It's like a compulsion to me to go and do it. I feel terrible about it, but I'm in a different world when I'm actually doing it…it's the challenge of doing it, I'm pitting my wits against their's, which really is a crummy thing to say when you're trying to pit your wits against a 60 or 70-year-old lady or something, it's a crummy thing to say. I dunno if I've got a conscience or not, cos I still keep going and doing it even though I think to myself, 'oh what a bastard' and that.

YLS [female aged 18]

When I was living in my mum's house, 'til I was about 14, there was me, my dad, my mum, my two brothers and my sister. Then my sister moved out; she's older than me, I'm the youngest in the family. My mum and dad got divorced when I was about 16, so dad moved out. One of my brothers moved out just after that, so in the end there was just me, my mum and one of my brothers. Mum and dad had steady jobs - mum was a cleaner, and dad was a painter and plasterer. He sometimes worked away on the oil rigs. He was working for someone but he was the boss of his men.

I lived in the same street all my life with my mum, then moved into my own place which is two or three minutes away from my mum's place; I've lived there for about a year now. I live in a three bed semi; it's my own council house, but I don't like it though, so I'm going to move. It's a nice house, but I don't feel comfortable in it; I've been burgled three or four times myself. The neighbours around there got involved in a lot of crime…burglaries, nicking cars, arson, assault. I knew this cos some of them I'd speak to, some of them were in the paper, others my friends would know…I'm fairly friendly with the neighbours where I am now. One of my neighbours gets involved with crime - things like burglaries, drugs. I know he's involved in burglaries as he's often offered me stuff.

The first thing I stole was clothes. The first time I did it I was 13. We, me and my friend, used to do it nearly every day. It was in [name of shop]. They had a corner of the shop which was really quiet - no cash tills or anything there, and there were loads of expensive blouses. So we used to get four or five of each blouse and sell them for about half price. I wasn't frightened…it was, like, 'oh, I'm young, I can't get into trouble.' We stole 15 blouses that first time. We always knew what we were going to do with the blouses before we took them - we'd sell them around where we lived.

I only ever got caught about two or three times out of 50. I did it about 10 times before I got caught. I never worried about getting caught. The first time I did get caught, I got put in cells. We'd stolen some clothes, I can't remember what exactly…I was nearly 14 then. It was the store detectives that caught us. I got bailed and a caution. At the caution, they just said 'don't do it again', and to be honest with you, I was nearly laughing...just a slap on the wrist, that's it. I thought they should have been harder on me. I carried on shoplifting the same day. At the time, when I was taking stuff, it didn't bother me. Most of the time when I did it, I'd say like, be running away from home and needing some money for food.

I never went to school. I started bunking off in the third year. I'd go one day a week or half day a week. The rest of the time I'd go into town. My mum knew I wasn't going to school. She got letters from the school, but in the end she just said 'oh, do what you like', lost her patience with me. My friend who I went shoplifting with and stuff bunked off school as well.

My mum didn't agree with what I was doing at first, but she knew I was doing it so she'd sometimes have the stuff. I'd sell it to her for about a quarter of the price. Sometimes she'd say that she needed a new skirt or something, we'd go out and get her it. She wouldn't say 'will you get me it', but if we had it she'd buy it, cos she's not one of those people that have got a lot of money. Mum didn't really agree with me doing it, but if I'd already done it, she'd buy it. Some of the neighbours would come up to me in the street and ask me to get them some baby clothes, or jeans, but that was more difficult.

I've never bought stolen goods - I've sold them, but never bought them myself. If there was something I wanted, I'd just go out and get it myself. Hardly ever bought my own clothes - just pinched them. If you get into it, it's hard to get out of...it's like an addiction, cos you just keep getting away with it or only getting a caution if you do get caught. I stopped shoplifting when I was 15 and a half. The stuff I nicked I sold around the estate.

I went into a kids' home when I was 14. I took overdoses to get out of the house, cos I was arguing with my dad. I got to the stage where I wasn't going to school at all...and I got put into care because of the overdoses. One of my brothers, he was doing something sexual to me...then my other brother started. I wanted to tell my mum, but like, it's her sons. So if I'd said 'they've been doing so and so to me, touching me', and she'd be like: 'oh, my son wouldn't do that'. So I was in two minds whether to tell her, even though she was my mum as well. I took an overdose and ended up in hospital. You always have to see a psychiatrist when you take an overdose. So I started speaking, letting it all out, and they brought the police in without me knowing, so I said about all the things that had happened like. They didn't put me in care that time. So I took another overdose. I took an overdose of paracetamol. The first time I only took about 25, the second time, the most I took was about 50. I only ended up in hospital for just a night - they gave me this brown stuff to drink what makes you sick, and they let me out the next day after I'd seen the psychiatrist. I always seemed to get caught out - somebody'd find the tablet bottle and I'd end up admitting I'd taken an overdose…I've got bad kidneys from it now.

The longest time I was in care for was about three months. I'd go back home, do runners, get into trouble…I went back home from care cos my mum would be saying, like: 'oh, come home'. Sometimes nothing happened to me, but I just couldn't take any more of being at home. I didn't get on with my dad…everything I did was wrong; he just used to get on me. I'd smash a car windscreen or something and go to a police station and say what I'd done so I'd get put in some cells. Then my mum and dad would refuse to have me home so I'd get put into care.

When they put me with foster parents, I wouldn't have it. Cos the foster parents I went to - they wanted to be mum and dad. And because of what happened at home, I didn't want a mum and dad. So I preferred it better in the children's home…I enjoyed it there. I didn't go to school when I was in the home. I'd already been expelled, so they like, got things from schools and made you do them there, things like Maths and English. They'd turn the tele off and that…and close the TV room and lock it, so you couldn't go in there at all during the day, so you'd do what somebody else would do at school. At night you had to be in bed by a certain time…it ranges for different ages. That's when I did my first burglary, in care. It was at a school, not my school. There was me, another girl, and two boys…we were all in care. To me, at the children's home, you had to fit in, if you didn't then you'd be the odd one out, and to me if I was the odd one out then I'd be like, being at home, cos then they might start picking on me and stuff like that. The lads suggested the break-in to the school. They picked up a bike-rack thing and put it through a window. We took a cash box with £2 or £3 in it, and went for a walk around the school. One of the lads wanted to take a violin, but I wouldn't let him…it was for little kids weren't it…I felt guilty about taking that.

I've done other burglaries, like, sneak-in burglaries - only houses that looked like they had loads of money - not ones where they didn't have much. What happens is, one person knocks on the front door, asks if so and so lived there, and the other person sneaks around the back and gets the purse. We only did it on big posh estates - big detached houses. We'd look for a house with no car in the drive - it's mainly males what drives cars, and if a male shuts the door on me and goes and catches my mate in the house, it'd be trouble. I never went in the house - I always knocked at the door. I didn't want anything to do with credit cards or cheque books or anything like that - just cash. They might be saving up money or something and I'd feel guilty. I know taking money was wrong, but credit cards and stuff seemed worse. I wish I'd never done it now, but like, I'm glad I did some of the things like getting put into care and that, cos I got out of the house, and with being in care you learn to grow up faster…more independent more quickly cos you're not living with your parents.

I did a lot of sneak-in burglaries, until we got caught. We only got caught for the one, and we'd done eight or nine that day. I was ready to admit that one to the police, but she, my mate, admitted all of them and said it was me that did it with her and that. I never actually got caught for the burglaries, I always got grassed up…the same girl grassed me up as I did the burglaries and stuff with. Say, if she got caught for something, she'd say 'oh I did this with so and so', so she'd get off with it, so I stopped doing things with her. We'd been doing it for a few months. I thought we were going to get sent down. That worried me because of the lesbians. I was used to my brothers and that punching me in the arms and legs and that when my mum and dad went out…I was quite scared of that, but I was more scared of the lesbians. I ended up in court, and got a supervision order. I had to go and see a sort of social worker/probation officer up until I was 17 and a half - that was two and a half years. I got involved in other stuff when I was on the supervision order, like nicking cars. I never drove the cars, I was always the passenger. The one time, the first time, I got into a stolen car we got caught. I did it a few more times after that. We didn't drive fast or nothing, just joyriding.

I haven't been in court now for three years, and the last time I was in court was for assault, cos this lass, when I was in the children's home, had been calling at me and saying that my mum goes out drinking every night and that. So I beat her, and then I found out that her dad was a vicar, so they took her side. But when I went to court I got off with it…that was when I was 16.

I get money from social at the moment, not managing on it, though. Got a loan for my house - for things like carpets, washer, baby's cot, bed. I was on £60. Now they've put me down to £40 a week because of the loan. So I've got to get my electric, gas, water rates, and get food out of that - and my baby's nappies.

I've got a one-year-old daughter now. I fell pregnant when I was 17 and a half…I haven't been in trouble since I had the baby. I still get offered stolen stuff now - videos and that, but, to me it's not worth it with me having a daughter and that. I got offered a video the other day, but I said no. I did have a video that we rented, but it got burgled. It is tempting to buy stolen stuff, cos it's cheap, but to me now, my daughter comes first rather than my own needs. It's risky, like, to buy stolen stuff, cos I don't know whether they'd grass me up or not. I want to buy it, but with my past record, if I got into trouble or anything, they'd probably bring the social workers in for my daughter. I'm not going to do it cos I've got too much to lose. Even when they come to me with baby clothes, I wouldn't buy them, cos it's my baby and I'd rather buy her stuff, cos when I buy her stuff, it makes me feel good…it's like buying presents for people, you feel good.

YOI [male aged 19]

I've lived in [name of town] all my life. I lived in…well, I did live…cos my mum's died now…in a three bedroom house…my step-dad lives there now with my baby sister and that. I get on better with him now that I don't live there. So at the moment, I've got no fixed address, well I have, I could go and live with my older sister when I get out, but no real fixed address. I was living with my girlfriend in [name of town] and her mum and dad and that, which is a block of flats on an estate. It's just down the road really from my mum's house. My dad's got a flat in [name of town] as well, so I've lived in [name of town] all my life.

I've got a lot of friends in this area. Everyone that I know is a bit bent, like, they'll buy stolen goods or they'll be on the thieve. There is a couple of my mates that are not into that. They'll buy stolen goods, but they'll hold down a job and do proper work with nice people. But most people I come into contact with is criminals.

My mum worked in a hi-fi shop down [name of town] and that. She was working there for a couple of years. See my mum's been dead three years this February…she died of lung cancer. My mum had a job all her life; she's always worked, never been in trouble with the police and that. She was always there for me. My step-dad, he don't smoke, drink…he works for the council, plays for a Sunday football team and that. He can't really understand why I get involved with crime. I've been inside before for burglary. My older brother, he's in prison now, he's done burglary as well. He's 25.

I've not really had a proper job since leaving school - I had sort of market jobs, but I can't say I've had a proper job. I work on market stalls that sell stuff like handbags, suitcases and that. I worked on a toiletries stall that was near enough full-time. I did a bit of that when I was at school. See, I was alright, I never missed a day at primary school. But when I went to secondary school I started bunking off. At first, like, I stopped going to lessons and then they sent a letter to my mum and that. Anyway, my mum's died of cancer now. But they sent letters to my mum and that. Then I just started playing truant and I mixed with the wrong crowd and that. And from there it started off with car radios, thieving things from cars; that was when I was about 14. Then it moved up from there.

The first things I bought that was stolen was a bit of jewellery. I was about 14. It was a bracelet that I bought for my girlfriend, and a sovereign ring. A friend offered it to me, a bit of an idiot, he sold me it cheap. I think it come out of a house; he'd stolen it. I paid about £30, silly money. I know jewellery shops that'll give me the proper money for it. I sold it on for one and a half, like, £150. What happened was, I gave the bracelet to my girlfriend then took it off her, cos I used to smoke a bit of charlie. I used to sniff a bit of cocaine and smoke crack, but not no more. She's still got a lot of stolen gold now.

I was 14 when I did my first burglary. I do burglaries cos it's a lot more money. It's like a buzz when I'm in the house cos I don't know what I'm finding. I don't ransack houses; I'll go through easy. I'll take the tele and the video, go in the bedroom, look in the drawer. I know it seems horrible, but like, it's like a buzz cos I dunno what I'm going to find, it's all little surprises I find. I get nervous all the time, looking about, thinking someone across the road might be watching me. I never do places when people are in. I have done creepers when I'm on crack, as in when people are asleep, like, and I've seen a window open…done that a few times. When I started, I had this mini. Me and my brother and my mate used to drive about in it. We mainly took TVs, videos, keyboards, stack systems, things like that. Sometimes we'd have to come back for a few loads. We took it down into a basement, into like, a little garage. We put it all in there. Then first thing in the morning, we shipped it out and sold it down the market. That'd be about 6 o'clock when people were setting up. Once we got our money we'd go and sleep all day.

I've bought stuff stolen quite a lot to sell on cos I can make more money on it. The police know it anyway, cos I've been nicked, loads of people have been nicked, down this market, just dodgy people selling stolen goods down there all the time. But when I was working down there, I used to have my friends come straight to me, to the market stall. And I'd buy the stuff off them and sell it to the other holders for top money. They'd come to me with teles, videos, in a cab round the back of the market and that. We'd do a deal, and I'll just take the stuff and put it down in the trailer, down the back like. I can clear the stuff like that, as soon as I've got it, it's gone. Everyone, anyone, down the market buys the stuff, the whole market knows who's going to buy it. Yeah, it's murder for teles, videos, camcorders and that. They're crying out for stuff like that. They give me quite a bit for it…whereas I'd pay fifty quid for a video, they'd give me a hundred pounds for it. I don't think they sell it, they keep it for themselves and that…nice little video present for their kid. They're not people that get in trouble with the police, they're just handlers. They get stuff for their friends, neighbours and that too. There's this geezer that I sell to at the top end of the market. I sell a lot of stuff to him cos sometimes it can be a bit of aggro going round all the market all the time. Sometimes I can't be bothered with all the others, so I just go to this geezer and get rid of it.

I was working on the market stall for about a year, every day. I'd have stolen stuff in the trailer every day, three or four times a day. I'd be making a lot of money in a week, over £1000. I'd spend that on clothes, designer clothes, jewellery. I got a car, things like that. I save some of it sometimes, that's how I got my car. I don't steal cars, I'm not into all that. I'll buy a car the natural way. I'll steal from cars. Never done any joyriding. My pals have and that, and like they say 'jump in and go for a ride', but I'm like, not into that, cos you don't earn no money out of that. And in the end, you get Old Bill chasing you…it ain't worth it.

People, like down the market and that, buy stuff off of me, off of my friends and that. But all they have to do is rip off the bit with the serial numbers on the back and that, and the police can't trace 'em back. Or they'll go out, they'll sell the stolen goods and with the money, buy receipted goods, so that way, they're legit, so when the Old Bill pick their house or whatever, they've got receipts. But then that stuff is bought with that stolen money. See, the police wouldn't expect that and as there's receipts there they can't do nothing. I've bought stolen goods once or twice. But I wouldn't really buy 'em cos I'd get 'em myself. But if I'd not been out there that day, like out there, I call it 'out there' when I'm on the thieve, and I see my friend and they've got a video to sell or something, they give it to me cheap. So yeah, I buy it off them and sell it for double that. But then the police come round my house and traced back the stolen stuff and that. So I'm like legit now. I'll sell the stolen goods and buy with the stolen money receipted goods. I won't have nothing stolen in my house. All my things get sold on.

I know a lot of people who are after stuff. I like to keep the flow, I like to keep it flowing. I don't like them to think, like, I'm slacking. I like to keep my person with stolen goods. I'd do it every day of the week, from about nine in the morning when everyone goes to work. I'd stay out 'til about four o'clock when most people start coming home. There's the odd day when I don't do it, like, when I get a lot of cash out of a house. Once I got £2,000, that lasted me a week, so I didn't have to go out for a week.

I knew when I stole the stuff who I was going to sell it to. My cassettes go to Turkish factories, that's one that makes clothes and all of that. My dad is Turkish, so I know a lot of these Turkish people that own factories and that. I go to them and sell car radios to them for top money. I got pals that own tele and video shops, and I'll sell 'em teles and videos. They'll clean it up and put it back up in the shop for proper money, £500 a video. I got friends that own car stereo shops as well. They sell straight as well as stolen stuff. But the customer won't know…as long as they get their receipt and that, and the things looking brand new…they just polish it up and that and change the serial number.

I've been caught cos of finger prints, apart from once when a geezer caught me in his house and cut me on the arm. I was in there unplugging his TV, when I heard footsteps so I looked round, and he's there in front of me in a towel. Anyway the police told me to make a statement, and all that. But what happened was, they took me out the back and arrested me for aggravated burglary, cos I'm known as a burglar and that. He said I pulled a Stanley knife on him in his house, so he's self defence when he used the knife on me, so he got off with it. I got charged with burglary in the end. If it had been me, if I caught someone doing my house, they would get it a lot worse. Thing is it didn't slow me down at all, just made me more alert. Since my mum died, my house has been burgled; it's never been burgled before. I know how it feels when people work hard for what they got and save up just to get a stack system, then you get someone go in and take their stuff.

I used to smoke, sniff, crack and things like that, just started doing it. Cos everyone goes partying and they sniff a bit of charlie and that. I just started getting bang on it, and really you could say it got to the point where I was going out there feeding my habit, cos I wouldn't have done eight, nine houses a day if it wasn't for that, but I wouldn't spend it all on crack, I'd go and buy clothes first, so I've got things to show for my money, then I'd go and buy charlie. Sometimes I'd swap stolen stuff for drugs, like when it's four o'clock in the morning and my Turkish factories aren't open yet. The drug dealers are out all night, see.

I don't take crack no more now, I'm frightened of it now. I can't go near crack again. And like my family, this is the last time my family is going to stick by me. If I go on it again I'll be a blown out junkie for the rest of my life, and I don't want that.

When I started doing car radios and that, I started selling cannabis, cutting it up and selling it up...and E's. But that's it really, but I don't touch that no more, cos of all the deaths and that. You don't make no money out of that anyway cos you take a couple of pills, and that's it, that's your profit you're taking.

My sister knows what's happening. She don't like it, she don't like it going on. My sister don't have nothing to do with stolen goods and that, she don't smoke, drink, no nothing. She's got two little girls, she's like into all that. But she knows it goes on all around her.

I've been in a YOI before, for two months, that was for burglary. I got caught on fingerprint evidence. It didn't make me stop. It's all about money, it's the only reason why I do it. Cos like, I've no qualifications or nothing. Like this time when I come out I want to sort myself out, I don't want to be doing it again. I'm going to try to stop. But there'll always be people looking for knocked off stuff. There'll always be handlers. If there wasn't these handlers, there wouldn't be no burglars.

REFERENCES

Baldwin, J. and Bottoms, A. (1976) *The Urban Criminal: a Study in Sheffield.* London: Tavistock.

Barr, R. and Pease, K. (1990) *Crime Placement, Displacement, and Deflection.* In Crime and Justice: A Review of Research, Vol 12, edited by Tonry, M. and Morris, N. Chicago: University of Chicago Press.

Bennett, J. (1981) *Oral History and Delinquency: The rhetoric of criminology.* The University of Chicago Press. Chicago.

Bennett, T. and Wright, R. (1984) *Burglars on Burglary: Prevention and the Offender.* Aldershot, UK: Gower.

Bennett, T. (1986) *Situational Crime Prevention from the Offender's Perspective.* In Situational Crime Prevention: from Theory into Practice. London: HMSO.

Benney, M. (1936) *Low Company: describing the evolution of a burglar.* London, Peter Davies.

Braithwaite, J. (1993) Beyond Positivism: Learning Contextual Integrated Strategies. *Journal of Research in Crime and Delinquency. 30/4: 389-99.*

Chambliss, W. J. (1984) *Harry King: a Professional Thief's Journey.* New York, John Wiley and Sons.

Clarke, R.V.G. (1983) Situational crime prevention: its theoretical basis and practical scope, in: Tonry, M. and Morris, N. (eds.) *Crime and Justice: An Annual Review of Research,* Vol 4. Chicago: University of Chicago Press.

Clarke, R.V.G. (1995) Situational Crime Prevention, in: Tonry, M. and Farrington, D. (Eds.) *Building a Safer Society: Strategic Approaches to Crime Prevention.* Vol 19. Crime and Justice. University of Chicago Press.

Cohen, A. (1955) *Delinquent Boys.* New York. Free Press.

Colquhoun, P. (1976) *A Treatise on The Police of the Metropolis.* London, C. Dilly.

Cromwell, P., Olson, J. and Avary, D. (1991) *Breaking and Entering: An Ethnographic Analysis of Burglary.* Sage. Calif.

Cromwell, P. and McElrath, K. (1994) Buying Stolen Property: An Opportunity Perspective. *Journal of Research in Crime and Delinquency, 31/ 3: 295-310.*

Cromwell, P. Olson, J. and Avery, D. (1993) *Who Buys Stolen Property? A new Look at Criminal Receiving.* Journal of Crime and Justice, Vol XVI, No 1.

Department of Social Security (1996) *Households Below Average Income: A statistical analysis 1979-1993/94.* London: The Stationery Office.

Edmunds, M., Hough, M. and Urquia, N. (1996) *Tackling Local Drug Markets.* Home Office Police Policy Directorate. Home Office. London.

Ekblom, P. (1988) *Getting the Best out of Crime Analysis.* Crime Prevention Unit Paper 10, HMSO.

Ekblom, P., Law, H. and Sutton, M. with Crisp, P. and Wiggins, R. (1996). *Domestic Burglary Schemes in the Safer Cities Programme.* Home Office Research Study No. 164. London. Home Office.

Ekblom, P. (1997). *Gearing Up Against Crime: a Dynamic Framework to Help Designers Keep up with the Adaptive Criminal in a Changing World.* International Journal of Risk, Security and Crime Prevention. October Issue.

Fattah, E. A. (1993) The Rational Choice/Opportunity Perspectives as a Vehicle for Integrating Criminological and Victimological Theories, in: R.V. Clarke and M. Felson (eds.), *Routine Activity and Rational Choice: Advances in Criminological Theory,* pp. 225-8. New Brunswick, NJ: Transactions Publishers.

Felson, M. (1994) *Crime and Everyday Life: Insights and Implications for Society.* California, Pine Forge Press.

Ferman, L. A., Henry, S. and Hoyman, M. (1987) *The Informal Economy.* Annals, AAPSS, Vol 493, September 1987. 154-172.

Ferrier, J. K. (1928) *Crooks and Crime: Describing the methods of* *criminals from the area to the professional card sharper forger or murderer and the various ways in which they are circumvented and captured.* London, Seeley, Service and Co Ltd.

Foster, J. (1990) *Villains: Crime and Community in the Inner City.* London: Routledge.

Foster, J. and Hope, T. and with the assistance of **Dowds, L. and Sutton, M.** (1993). *Housing, Community and Crime: The Impact of the Priority Estates Project.* Home Office Research Study 131, Home Office, London.

Frisbie, D. (1982) *Crime Analysis is Crime Prevention Planning,* 530-558 in: Fennelly, L. (ed) *Handbook of Loss Prevention and Crime Prevention.* Butterworths. Boston.

Goodman, A. and Webb, S. (1995). *The Distribution of Household Expenditure, 1979-92.* The Institute for Fiscal Studies. Commentary No.49.

Goodman, A., Johnson, P. and Webb, S. (1997). Inequality in the UK. Oxford. Oxford University Press.

Graham, J. and Bennett, T. (1995) *Crime Prevention Strategies in Europe and North America.* European Institute for Crime Prevention and Control. Publication series No. 28.

Graham, J. and Bowling, B. (1995) *Young people and Crime.* Home Office Research Study 145, Home Office, London.

Gregory, J. (1932) *Crime from the Inside: Revelations and Confessions of Warder, Confidence Trickster and "Fence".* London, John Long Ltd.

Hall, J. (1952) *Theft, Law and Society.* 2nd ed. Indianapolis: Bobbs-Merrill Co.

Heiner, W. and Heiner, J. (eds.) (1968) *A Burglar's Life.* Sydney, Australia. Angus and Robertson.

Hobbs, D. (1989) **Doing the Business: Entrepreneurship, The Working Class and Detectives in the East End of London.** Oxford: Oxford University Press.

Hough, M. (1984) Residential Burglary: Findings from the British Crime Survey, in: R.V.G. Clarke and M. Felson (eds.) *Routine Activities and Rational Choice: Advances in Criminological Theory.* New Brunswick, NJ: Transactions Publishers.

Hough, M. (1995) *Anxiety about Crime: Findings from the 1994 British Crime Survey.* Home Office Research Study no 147, Home Office, London..

Jochelson, R. (1995) Household break-ins and the market for stolen goods. *Crime and Justice Bulletin, No 24.* New South Wales Bureau of Crime Statistics and Research.

Johnson, D., Mangai, N. and Sanabria, H. (1993) 'Successful' Criminal Careers: Towards an Ethnography within the Rational Choice Perspective. In Clarke, R. V. and Felson, M. *Routine Activity and Rational Choice: Advances in Criminological Theory.* New Brunswick: Transactions Publishers.

Klockars, C. (1974) *The Professional Fence.* New York. Free Press.

Knutsson, J. (1984) *Operation Identification: a way to prevent burglaries?* The National Council for Crime Prevention Sweden. Research Division. Stockholm. Report No 14.

Kock, E., Kemp, T. and Rix, B. (1996) *Disrupting the Distribution of Stolen Electrical Goods.* Home Office Police Department.

Laycock, G. (1985) *Property Marking: A Deterrent to Domestic Burglary?* Home Office Crime Prevention Unit Paper 3. Home Office, London.

Leitch, D. (1969) *The Discriminating Thief.* London, Hodder and Stoughton.

Levi, M. Bissell, P. and Richardson, T. (1991) *The Prevention of Cheque and Credit Card Fraud.* Crime Prevention Unit paper 26. Home Office, London.

Light, R., Nee, C. and Ingham, H. (1993). *Car theft: the offender's perspective.* A Home Office Research and Planning Unit Report, Home Office, London.

Lloyd, C., Mair, G. and Hough M. (1994) *Explaining reconviction rates: a critical analysis.* A Home Office Research and Planning Unit Report, London, HMSO.

Maguire, M. in collaboration with **Bennett, T.** (1982) *Burglary in a Dwelling: the Offence, the Offender and the Victim.* London, Heinemann.

Mayhew, P., Clarke, R. V., Sturmann, A. and Hough, J. M. (1976) *Crime as Opportunity.* A Home Office Research Study, No 34. London, HMSO.

Mayhew, P., Elliott, D. and Dowds, L. (1989) *The 1988 British Crime Survey.* Home Office Research Study No 111. London, HMSO.

Mayhew, P., Aye Maung, N. and Mirrlees-Black, C. (1993) *The 1992 British Crime Survey.* Home Office Research Study No 132. London, HMSO.

Mirrlees-Black, C., Mayhew, P. and Percy, A. (1996) *The 1996 British Crime Survey: England and Wales.* Home Office Statistical Bulletin, Issue 19/96.

Munro, A. K. (1972) *Autobiography of a Thief.* London, Michael Joseph.

Nee, C. and Taylor, M. (1988) Residential Burglary in the Republic of Ireland: A Situational Perspective. *The Howard Journal* Vol 27 No 2.

Norusis, M. J. (1990) *The SPSS Advanced Statistics Student Guide.* SPSS International, Chicago Illinois.

Park, R., Burgess, E. and Mckenzie, R. (1925) *The City.* Chicago: University of Chicago Press.

Parker, H. (1974) *View From The Boys: a Sociology of Down Town Adolescents.* David and Charles.

Parker, H., Bakx, K. and Newcombe, R. (1988) *Living with Heroin: The Impact of a Drugs 'epidemic' on an English Community.* Milton Keynes: OUP.

Parker, H. and Bottomley, T. (1996) *Crack Cocaine and Drugs-Crime Careers.* Home Office, London.

Pawson, R. and Tilley, N. (1994). What Works in Evaluation Research. British *Journal of Criminology, Vol 34, No 1 pp 291-306.*

Pengelly, R. (1996) *The Black Economy Boom.* Police Review, 14 December.

Quennell, P. (1962) *London's Underworld.* London, Spring Books.

Ramsay, M. and Percy, A. (1996) *Drug misuse declared: results of the 1994 British Crime Survey.* A Research and Statistics Directorate Report. Home Office, London.

Reuter, P. (1985) *The Organization of Illegal Markets: An Economic Analysis.* National Institute of Justice. US Department of Justice.

Reuter, P. (1990) *Money From Crime: A Study of the Economics of Drug Dealing in Washington DC.* RAND Corporation: Drug Policy Research Centre.

Roselius, T. and Benton, D. (1973) Marketing Theory and the Fencing of Stolen Goods. *Denver Law Journal, 50: 177-205.*

Sarnecki, J. (1986) *Delinquent Networks.* National Council for Crime Prevention. Stockholm, Sweden.

Shaw, H. and McKay, H. D. (1942) Juvenile Delinquency in Urban Areas. Chicago. University of Chicago Press.

Shover, N. (1972) Structures and Careers in Burglary. *The Journal of Criminal Law, Criminology and Police Science. Vol 63, No. 4: 540-449*

Shover, N. (1996) *The Great Pretenders: Pursuits and Careers of Persistent Thieves.* Westview Press.

Smithies, E. (1984) *The Black Economy in England since 1914.* Gill and Macmillan Humanities Press, Goldenbridge, Dublin, Ireland.

Steffensmeier, D. J. (1986) *The Fence: In the Shadow of Two Worlds.* New Jersey: Rowman and Littlefield.

Stockdale, J.E. and Gresham, P.J. (1995) *Combating Burglary: An Evaluation of Three Strategies.* Police Research Group, Crime Detection and Prevention Series: Paper No 59, London: Home Office Police Department.

Stone, J. (1975) *The Burglars Bedside Companion.* London: Everest.

Sutton, M. (1993). From Receiving to Thieving: the market for stolen goods and the incidence of theft. *Home Office Research Bulletin, No. 34*

Sutton, M. (1995) Supply by Theft: does the market for second-hand goods play a role in keeping crime figures high. *British Journal of Criminology, Vol 38 No. 3 Summer 1995.*

Sutton, M. (1996) *Implementing crime prevention schemes in a multi-agency setting: aspects of process in the Safer Cities programme.* Home Office Research Study 160.

Sykes, G. and Matza, D. (1957) Techniques of Neutralization: A Theory of Delinquency, *American Sociological Review,* 22 December, pp. 664-70.

Tilley, N. (1992) *Safer Cities and Community Safety Strategies.* Police Research Group, Crime Prevention Unit Series: No 38, London, HMSO.

Tilley, N. Realism, Situational Rationality and Crime Prevention, in: Newman, G., Clarke, R. V. and Shoham, S. G. (1997). *Rational Choice and Situational Crime Prevention.* Aldershot, Ashgate.

Tobias, J. (1974) *Prince of Fences.* London, Valentine Mitchell.

Tremblay, P., Clermont, Y. and Cusson, M. (1994) Jockeys and Joyriders: Changing Patterns in Car Theft Opportunity Structures. *British Journal of Criminology, Vol 34 No. 3 Summer 1994. 307-321.*

Trickett, A., Ellingworth, D., Hope, T. and Pease, K. (1995) Crime Victimization in the Eighties: Changes in Area and Regional Inequality. *British Journal of Criminology,* Vol 35. No. 3 Summer 1995. 342-359.

Walker, M. (1983) Self Reported Crime Studies and the British Crime Survey. The Howard Journal, Vol XXII, pp 168-176.

Walsh, M. (1977) *The Fence: A new Look at the World of Property Theft.* Connecticut. Greenwood Press.

Ward, D. (1989) *King of the Lags: The Story of Charles Peace.* London, Souvenir Press.

West, D. J. (1982) *Delinquency: its Roots Careers and Prospects.* London: Heinemann.

Wright, T. and Decker, S. H. (1994) *Burglars on the Job: Streetlife and Residential Break-ins.* Boston. Northeastern University Press.

Publications

List of research publications

A list of research reports for the last three years is provided below. A **full** list of publications is available on request from the Research and Statistics Directorate Information and Publications Group.

Home Office Research Studies (HORS)

151. **Drug misuse declared: results of the 1994 British Crime Survey.** Malcolm Ramsay and Andrew Percy. 1996.

152. **An Evaluation of the Introduction and Operation of the Youth Court.** David O'Mahony and Kevin Haines. 1996.

153. **Fitting supervision to offenders: assessment and allocation decisions in the Probation Service.** 1996.

155. **PACE: a review of the literature. The first ten years.** David Brown. 1997.

156. **Automatic Conditional Release: the first two years.** Mike Maguire, Brigitte Perroud and Peter Raynor. 1996.

157. **Testing obscenity: an international comparison of laws and controls relating to obscene material.** Sharon Grace. 1996.

158. **Enforcing community sentences: supervisors' perspectives on ensuring compliance and dealing with breach.** Tom Ellis, Carol Hedderman and Ed Mortimer. 1996.

159. is not published yet.

160. **Implementing crime prevention schemes in a multi-agency setting: aspects of process in the Safer Cities programme.** Mike Sutton. 1996.

161. **Reducing criminality among young people: a sample of relevant programmes in the United Kingdom.** David Utting. 1997.

162. **Imprisoned women and mothers.** Dianne Caddle and Debbie Crisp. 1996.

163. **Curfew orders with electronic monitoring: an evaluation of the first twelve months of the trials in Greater Manchester, Norfolk and Berkshire, 1995 - 1996.** George Mair and Ed Mortimer. 1996..

164. **Safer cities and domestic burglaries.** Paul Ekblom, Ho Law, Mike Sutton, with assistance from Paul Crisp and Richard Wiggins. 1996.

165. **Enforcing financial penalties.** Claire Whittaker and Alan Mackie. 1997.

166. **Assessing offenders' needs: assessment scales for the probation service.** Rosumund Aubrey and Michael Hough. 1997.

167. **Offenders on probation.** George Mair and Chris May. 1997.

168. **Managing courts effectively: The reasons for adjournments in magistrates' courts.** Claire Whittaker, Alan Mackie, Ruth Lewis and Nicola Ponikiewski. 1997.

169. **Addressing the literacy needs of offenders under probation supervision.** Gwynn Davis et al. 1997.

170. **Understanding the sentencing of women.** Edited by Carol Hedderman and Lorraine Gelsthorpe. 1997.

171. **Changing offenders' attitudes and behaviour: what works?** Julie Vennard, Darren Sugg and Carol Hedderman 1997.

172. **Drug misuse declared in 1996: latest results from the British Crime Survey.** Malcolm Ramsay and Josephine Spiller. 1997.

Research Findings

30. **To scare straight or educate? The British experience of day visits to prison for young people.** Charles Lloyd. 1996.

31. **The ADT drug treatment programme at HMP Downview – a preliminary evaluation.** Elaine Player and Carol Martin. 1996.

32. **Wolds remand prison – an evaluation.** Keith Bottomley, Adrian James, Emma Clare and Alison Liebling. 1996.

33. **Drug misuse declared: results of the 1994 British Crime Survey.** Malcolm Ramsay and Andrew Percy. 1996.

34. **Crack cocaine and drugs-crime careers.** Howard Parker and Tim Bottomley. 1996.

35. **Imprisonment for fine default.** David Moxon and Claire Whittaker. 1996.

36. **Fine impositions and enforcement following the Criminal Justice Act 1993.** Elizabeth Charman, Bryan Gibson, Terry Honess and Rod Morgan. 1996.

37. **Victimisation in prisons.** Ian O'Donnell and Kimmett Edgar. 1996.

38. **Mothers in prison.** Dianne Caddle and Debbie Crisp. 1997.

39. **Ethnic minorities, victimisation and racial harassment.** Marian Fitzgerald and Chris Hale. 1996.

40. **Evaluating joint performance management between the police and the Crown Prosecution Service.** Andrew Hooke, Jim Knox and David Portas. 1996.

41. **Public attitudes to drug-related crime.** Sharon Grace. 1996.

42. **Domestic burglary schemes in the safer cities programme.** Paul Ekblom, Ho Law and Mike Sutton. 1996.

43. **Pakistani women's experience of domestic violence in Great Britain.** Salma Choudry. 1996.

44. **Witnesses with learning disabilities.** Andrew Sanders, Jane Creaton, Sophia Bird and Leanne Weber. 1997.

45. **Does treating sex offenders reduce reoffending?** Carol Hedderman and Darren Sugg. 1996.

46. **Re-education programmes for violent men - an evaluation.** Russell Dobash, Rebecca Emerson Dobash, Kate Cavanagh and Ruth Lewis. 1996.

47. **Sentencing without a pre-sentence report.** Nigel Charles, Claire Whittaker and Caroline Ball. 1997.

48. **Magistrates' views of the probation service.** Chris May. 1997.

49. **PACE ten years on: a review of the research.** David Brown. 1997.

50. **Persistent drug–misusing offenders.** Malcolm Ramsay. 1997.

51. **Curfew orders with electronic monitoring: The first twelve months.** Ed Mortimer and George Mair. 1997.

52. **Police cautioning in the 1990s.** Roger Evans and Rachel Ellis. 1997.

53. **A reconviction study of HMP Grendon Therapeutic Community.** Peter Marshall. 1997.

54. **Control in category c prisons.** Simon Marshall. 1997.

55. **The prevalence of convictions for sexual offending.** Peter Marshall. 1997.

56. **Drug misuse declared in 1996: key results from the British Crime Survey.** Malcolm Ramsay and Josephine Spiller. 1997.

57. **The 1996 International Crime Victimisation Survey.** Pat Mayhew and Phillip White. 1997.

58. **The sentencing of women: a section 95 publication.** Carol Hedderman and Lizanne Dowds. 1997.

Occasional Papers

Mental disorder in remand prisoners. Anthony Maden, Caecilia J. A. Taylor, Deborah Brooke and John Gunn. 1996.

An evaluation of prison work and training. Frances Simon and Claire Corbett. 1996.

The impact of the national lottery on the horse-race betting levy. Simon Field. 1996.

Evaluation of a Home Office initiative to help offenders into employment. Ken Roberts, Alana Barton, Julian Buchanan, and Barry Goldson. 1997.

The impact of the national lottery on the horse-race betting levy. Simon Field and James Dunmore. 1997.

Requests for Publications

Home Office Research Studies from 143 onwards, *Research and Planning Unit Papers, Research Findings and Research Bulletins* can be requested, **subject to availability**, from:

Research and Statistics Directorate
Information and Publications Group
Room 201, Home Office
50 Queen Anne's Gate
London SW1H 9AT
Telephone: 0171-273 2084
Facsimile: 0171-222 0211
Internet: http://www.open.gov.uk/home off/rsd/rsdhome.htm
E-mail: rsd.ha apollo @ gtnet.gov.u.

Occasional Papers can be purchased from:
Home Office
Publications Unit
50 Queen Anne's Gate
London SW1H 9AT
Telephone: 0171 273 2302

Home Office Research Studies prior to 143 can be purchased from:

The Publications Centre

(Mail, fax and telephone orders only)
PO Box 276, London SW8 5DT
Telephone orders: 0171-873 9090
General enquiries: 0171-873 0011
(queuing system in operation for both numbers)
Fax orders: 0171-873 8200

*And also from **Stationery Office Bookshops***